# THE
# HISTORY
# OF
# SCIENCE

# THE
# HISTORY
## OF
# SCIENCE

EDITED BY HOPE MERLIN

**Britannica**
Educational Publishing

IN ASSOCIATION WITH

**ROSEN**
EDUCATIONAL SERVICES

Published in 2014 by Britannica Educational Publishing (a trademark of Encyclopædia Britannica, Inc.) in association with The Rosen Publishing Group, Inc.
29 East 21st Street, New York, NY 10010

Distributed exclusively by Rosen Publishing.
To see additional Britannica Educational Publishing titles, go to rosenpublishing.com.

First Edition

Britannica Educational Publishing
J.E. Luebering: Director, Core Reference Group
Anthony L. Green: Editor, Compton's by Britannica

Rosen Educational Services
Hope Lourie Killcoyne: Executive Editor
Nelson Sá: Art Director
Nelson Sá: Designer
Cindy Reiman: Photography Manager
Nicole Baker: Photo Researcher
Introduction by Adam Augustyn

**Library of Congress Cataloging-in-Publication Data**

Merlin, Hope.
The history of science/[edited by] Hope Merlin. – First edition.
    pages cm. – (Scientific inquiry: concepts, methods, and theories)
Audience: Grades 9-12.
Includes bibliographical references and index.
ISBN 978-1-62275-116-7 (library binding)
1. Science–History–Juvenile literature. I. Killcoyne, Hope Lourie, editor. II. Title.
Q125.H633 2014
509–dc23
                                                                    2013022941

*Manufactured in the United States of America*

**On the cover, p. iii:** Polish astronomer Nicolaus Copernicus, who theorized that the Earth and other planets revolve around the Sun, is often considered the founder of modern astronomy. *Universal Images Group/Getty Images*

Cover and interior pages (microscope) janrysavy/iStockphoto.com; interior pages background images © cosmin4000/iStockphoto.com, © Sergey Nivens/iStockphoto.com, © mstay/iStockphoto.com

# CONTENTS

**10**

**23**

**38**

43

57

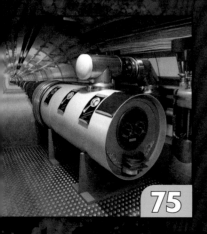
75

Like all other fields of academic study, science has evolved over time as its practitioners made new discoveries building upon those of their predecessors. This practice has produced a long and convoluted history of scientific advances over the centuries, filled with countless starts and stops. In fact, the history of science is even older than writing itself, as early humans participated in nascent scientific endeavours by tracking the movements of the Sun and the Moon and noting how these affected their lives through—among other phenomena—the fluctuations of daylight and seasons. However, these recognitions of cosmic regularities were not truly scientific enterprises, which require an investigation into the causes of observed natural phenomena. Early *Homo sapiens* were content simply to note these movements and chalk the agency up to the whims of the gods.

Among the first recorded human activities of scientific importance are the European megalithic structures,

*Overhead view of the prehistoric monument known as Stonehenge.* George W. Bailey/Shutterstock.com

such as Stonehenge in Great Britain, that were erected around 2500 BCE. The massive rock formations appear to have served both religious and astronomical purposes. Religion and astronomy were practically interchangeable in many of the earliest human civilizations, including Egypt, Mesopotamia, and Central America, since the movements of heavenly objects were understandably assumed to be the direct work of deities to those in pre-technological times. The fusion of religion to astronomy made the latter the leading science throughout human civilization for the following 4,000 years.

The ritual dimension of religion-based astronomy helped stimulate the rise of mathematics, as early astronomers developed the science to plot and, later, predict the regular movement of stars and planets. In ancient China, astronomy-derived math was used to create one of the first accurate calendars, which was thoroughly integrated into the complex Chinese bureaucracy from the 2nd millennium BCE. The need for even more detailed calendars gave rise to more precise astronomical observations over the years, which helped lay the groundwork for the emphasis on the practicality of ancient China's scientific advances, which included landmark developments in medicine, geology, geography, and alchemy.

Another locale notable for its early scientific advances was Mesopotamia. Like China, there was a practical aspect to the scientific developments in Mesopotamia: living in the region was dependent on harnessing the Tigris and Euphrates rivers—as well as on avoiding the many storms, floods, and invaders that plagued the area—and the need to create a stable society in such an unpredictable environment fed the technological advancement of its inhabitants. Necessity, as they say, is the mother of invention. Mesopotamians thus made great strides in mathematics and astronomy, including noteworthy developments in what would become algebra and elaborately describing astronomical movements. While Chinese and Mesopotamian civilizations produced theretofore unrecorded descriptions of nature, their developments still lacked the reasoned descriptions of proper science and were instead seen as functions of religion and magic. The first civilization to attempt to find explanations of natural phenomena outside of the arbitrary will of the gods was ancient Greece.

One of the key reasons for the different approaches to science of Greece and of earlier civilizations is the Greeks' relationship with their gods. The ancient Greek religion contained oft-childish gods who knew no better than the humans they interacted with, and these interactions were collected in what were essentially folk tales, which were primarily literary works and were not intended to answer people's questions about their place in the world. Thus, the Greeks did not have any easy theological explanations as to what underpinned natural phenomena, which led Greek thinkers to rely on reasoning when contemplating the world, resulting in the advent of both philosophy and the precursor to modern science, natural philosophy.

Thales of Miletus is traditionally considered to be the first natural philosopher. He theorized that all natural phenomena derive from one of the three states of water. This theory was especially notable in that it proposed that regularity and rationality—not supernatural whims—govern the world, which later gave rise to the two fundamental Greek scientific characteristics: the universe is ordered and all parts of it have a purpose in the grand scheme of things. The latter notion, known as teleology, would go on to be a key (though ultimately unfounded) part of scientific theories through the 19th century. Thales made another signature contribution to the history of science by the simple act of naming a specific entity that underlay all matter, which left his opinion open to critiques by his disciple Anaximander and gave birth to the cycle of criticism and revision that is a central feature of scientific advances.

While Thales' contributions to science were notable for what they initiated, the findings themselves have not stood the test of time. The same cannot be said of the works of his fellow Greek natural philosophers Aristotle and Archimedes. Aristotle is best known for his contributions to the development of philosophy, but his work in biology served as the foundation of that science until the Darwinian biological revolution. In addition, he initiated the Greek tradition (and that of many subsequent ancient civilizations) of relying solely on observation, as opposed to experimentation, to investigate the world. Archimedes' contributions to mathematics laid the groundwork for the advent of calculus, and his pioneering demonstration that physical characteristics can be represented and manipulated in a mathematical manner. Another noteworthy Greek scientific advance internalized—quite literally—the exterior forces that previous civilizations thought governed the natural world, as Hippocrates asserted that maladies originated inside the body, setting the course for all future medical progress.

With the exception of the monumental advances of early Islamic scientists (notably the invention of algebra), the development of science was largely stagnant after the decline of ancient Greek civilization until the medieval era. Despite being later denigrated by Enlightenment writers as the "Dark Ages," the Middle Ages were in fact a time of advances that have become so fundamental that later scientists could not gloss over their importance. Among the many important inventions to come out of the Middle Ages are horseshoes, the crank, the flying buttress, windmills, and the wheelbarrow. While medieval scientists still believed (like their Islamic forebears) that a paranormal force, namely the God of the modern monotheistic religions, was ultimately responsible for all natural phenomena, there nevertheless was no purposeful conflict between religion and science at the time. Instead, medieval scientists followed the lead of the philosopher Thomas Aquinas, who believed that since God created both nature and scripture, which each required investigation and interpretation by man, then science and religion were essentially two sides of the same coin.

The medieval integration of science and religion was slowly unraveled during the most important movement in the history of science, which has become known, appropriately enough, as the scientific revolution. The movement originated in the explosion of antiquity-inspired intellectual activity of the Renaissance, which began in different locations throughout Europe between 1200 and 1400. The most important scientific developments of the Renaissance were the astronomical discoveries of Nicolaus Copernicus, Tycho Brahe, Johannes Kepler, and Galileo Galilei. Copernicus fired the first shots at the millennium-old assumption that the Earth was the centre of the universe when he revealed in his book *De revolutionibus orbium coelestium libri VI* ("Six Books Concerning the Revolutions of the Heavenly Orbs") that his precise mathematical and observational efforts proved that the Sun was instead the centre of the known cosmos. Placing the Earth into orbit around the Sun led to another profound revelation: since the positions of the stars do not shift as the Earth revolves around the Sun—as would be expected if the stars were relatively close to Earth—Copernicus showed that the universe was far larger than had been previously thought. These twin disclosures wreaked havoc on the traditional Judeo-Christian concept of the cosmos: if man was indeed God's most important creation, why would God bother to produce so much more and make the Earth such a minor part of the universe? Copernicus created a critical tradition that continued on in the work of Tycho, who produced the most accurate planetary and stellar measurements of his time; Kepler, whose discovery of the elliptical orbits of planets filled one of the key gaps in the Copernican theory; and Galileo, whose telescopic observations discovered numerous heavenly bodies that devastated the concept of universal perfection that held sway since the days of Aristotle. As a whole, the work of the four astronomers instigated a sea change in the fundamental way man viewed his relationship with the world around him, the importance of which cannot be overstated.

The terrestrial analogue of these celestial findings came in the work of Isaac Newton. He made incredibly important strides in the field of calculus, but he is best known for his contributions to physics. Newton discovered the three basic laws of motion that define how forces act on a body and how that body subsequently moves. His laws applied to celestial bodies as well as to Earth-bound objects and they served as the building blocks for modern mechanical physics. (However, in the 20th century, quantum physics and relativity replaced Newton's laws as the most fundamental laws of physics; Newton's laws continue to yield accurate measures of natural phenomena, except for small bodies such as electrons and for bodies moving near the speed of light.) In addition, Newton's 1704 masterpiece *Opticks* became one of the most important works of experimental physics, as it showed that thorough experimental examinations can produce findings that simple observations cannot. The treatise helped to the now-standard scientific method of repeate hypotheses with experimental investigation unt theory can be made.

The experimental approaches of Newton (and other scientists) continued to bear fruit throughout the 18th and 19th centuries. Antoine-Laurent Lavoisier initiated a chemical revolution when he experimentally proved that oxygen, and not the pseudoscientific substance phlogiston, was the key to combustion. He also stressed that precise analysis was the key concern of the new chemistry he established. Lavoisier's groundbreaking findings were followed by similarly important discoveries by Michael Faraday (whose work with electric currents later led to the establishment of field theory) and John Dalton (the originator of the atomic theory).

Of course, observation still played an important role in scientific advances. Arguably the most extraordinary theory to come from observing natural phenomena was Charles Darwin's theory of evolution. After many years of painstakingly observing the natural variation of organisms, Darwin deduced that these differences came into being over long periods of time as species adapted and took on new forms, establishing the theory that all life was not divinely created but instead evolved from previous living beings. As the work of Copernicus created doubt as to man's role in God's great plan, Darwin's theory rocked the foundations of man's self-regard, bringing the very existence of God into question.

While the 1800s were broadly thought of as the century of chemistry (with the advent of atomic theory and the periodic table of elements, among other landmark breakthroughs) and the 1900s were the era of physics (marked primarily by Einstein's theory of relativity and the subsequent developments of the atomic bomb and nuclear

energy), the 21st century has been predicted by some science writers as potentially being the century of biology.
Late 20th- and early 21st-century developments such as
animal cloning, the mapping of the human genome, and
the rise of genetically modified organisms (GMOs) have
poised biologists to affect the human experience to as
large a degree as those earlier upheavals had.

Of course, the history of science is not complete—
the investigation into the natural laws continues to this
day. As long as more and more natural phenomena are
exposed to the human senses through technological
advances and innovative methods of investigation, scientists will persist in making new and sometimes seemingly
shocking discoveries. Perhaps the best example of this in
the contemporary world is the rapid innovation seen
in computer technology. As seen in the evolution of large
and slow desktop computers to lightning-fast laptops,
which were in turn complemented and superseded by
tablets and smartphones, the march of scientific progress
continues apace, which will undoubtedly lead to future
generations recording modern advancements in the book
of science history.

# SCIENCE AS NATURAL PHILOSOPHY

O n the simplest level, science is knowledge of the world of nature. There are many regularities in nature that mankind has had to recognize for survival since the emergence of *Homo sapiens* as a species. The Sun and the Moon periodically repeat their movements. Some motions, such as the daily "motion" of the Sun, are simple to observe; others, such as the annual "motion" of the Sun, are far more difficult. Both motions correlate with important terrestrial events. Day and night provide the basic rhythm of human existence; the seasons determine the migration of animals upon which humans have depended for millennia for survival. With the invention of agriculture, the seasons became even more crucial, for failure to recognize the proper time for planting could lead to starvation. Science defined simply as knowledge of natural processes is universal among human beings, and it has existed since the dawn of our existence.

The mere recognition of regularities does not exhaust the full meaning of science, however. In the first place, regularities may be simply constructs of the human mind. Humans leap to conclusions; the mind cannot tolerate chaos, so it creates regularities even when none objectively exists. Thus, for example, one of the astronomical "laws" of the Middle Ages was that the appearance of comets presaged a great upheaval, as the Norman Conquest of Britain followed the comet of 1066. True regularities must be established by detached examination of data. Science, therefore, must employ a certain degree of skepticism to prevent premature generalization.

Regularities, even when expressed mathematically as laws of nature, are not fully satisfactory to everyone. Some insist that genuine understanding demands explanations of the causes of the laws, but it is in the realm of causation that there is the greatest disagreement. Modern quantum mechanics, for example, has given up the quest for causation and today rests only on mathematical description. Modern biology, on the other hand, thrives on causal chains that permit the understanding of physiological and evolutionary processes in terms of the physical activities of entities such as molecules, cells, and organisms. But even if causation and explanation are admitted as necessary, there is little agreement on the kinds of causes that are permissible, or possible, in science. If the history of science is to make any sense whatsoever, it is necessary to deal with the past on its own terms, and the fact is that for most of the history of science natural philosophers appealed to causes that would be summarily rejected by modern scientists. Spiritual and divine forces were accepted as both real and necessary until the end of the 18th century and, in areas such as biology, deep into the 19th century as well.

Certain conventions governed the appeal to God or the gods or to spirits. Gods and spirits, it was held, could not be completely arbitrary in their actions; otherwise the proper response would be atonement not rational investigation. But since the deity or deities were themselves rational, or bound by rational principles, it was possible for humans to uncover the rational order of the world. Faith in the ultimate rationality of the creator or governor of the world could actually stimulate original scientific work. Kepler's laws, Newton's absolute space, and Einstein's rejection of the probabilistic nature of quantum mechanics were all based on theological, not scientific, assumptions. For sensitive interpreters of phenomena, the ultimate intelligibility of nature has seemed to demand some rational guiding spirit. A notable expression of this idea is Einstein's statement that the wonder is not that mankind comprehends the world, but that the world is comprehensible.

Science, then, is to be considered in this book as knowledge of natural regularities that is subjected to some degree of skeptical rigour and explained by rational causes. One final caution is necessary. Nature is known only through the senses, of which sight, touch, and hearing are the dominant ones, and the human notion of reality is skewed toward the objects of these senses. The invention of such instruments as the telescope, the microscope, and the Geiger counter has brought an ever-increasing range of phenomena within the range of the senses. Thus, scientific knowledge of the world is only partial, and the progress of science follows the ability of humans to make phenomena perceivable.

This book provides a broad survey of the development of science as a way of studying and understanding the world, from the primitive stage of noting important regularities in nature to the epochal revolution in our notion of what constitutes reality that has occurred in modern science.

# PRECRITICAL SCIENCE

Science, as it has been defined earlier, made its appearance before writing. It is necessary, therefore, to infer from archaeological remains what was the content of that science. From cave paintings and from apparently regular scratches on bone and reindeer horn, it is known that prehistoric humans were close observers of nature who carefully tracked the seasons and times of the year. About 2500 BCE there was a sudden burst of activity that seems to have had clear scientific importance. Great Britain and northwestern Europe contain large stone structures from that era, the most famous of which is Stonehenge on the Salisbury Plain in England, that are remarkable from a scientific point of view. Not only do they reveal technical and social skills of a high order—it was no mean feat to move such enormous blocks of stone considerable distances and place them in position—but the basic conception of Stonehenge and the other megalithic structures also seems to combine

*Poulnabrone Dolmen, a prehistoric megalithic tomb in County Clare, Ireland.* Holger Leue/Tourism Ireland

# MEGALITHIC MONUMENTS

Megaliths are huge, often undressed stone used in various types of Neolithic (New Stone Age) and Early Bronze Age monuments.

Although some aspects of the spread and development of megalithic monuments are still under debate, in Spain, Portugal, and the Mediterranean coast the most ancient of the cyclopean stone tombs was probably the dolmen. The dolmen consisted of several upright supports and a flat roofing slab, all covered by a protective mound of earth that in most cases has weathered away. In northern and western Europe, two principal plans developed from the dolmen: one, the passage grave, was formed by the addition of a long stone-roofed entrance passage to the dolmen itself; and the other, the long, coffinlike cist or covered gallery grave, consisted of a long, rectangular burial chamber with no distinct passageway. Hybrid versions have also been discovered, for example, in the Hebrides, a group of islands off the west coast of Scotland. Many round and long barrows also were found to contain megalithic burial chambers.

Another form of the megalithic monument was the menhir (from Breton *men*, "stone," and *hir*, "long"), which may or may not occur in connection with a megalithic grave. Menhirs were simple upright stones, sometimes of great size, and were erected most frequently in western Europe, especially Brittany. Often menhirs were placed together, forming circles, semicircles, or vast ellipses. Many were built in England, the best-known sites being Stonehenge and Avebury in Wiltshire. Megalithic menhirs were also placed in several parallel rows, called alignments. The most famous of these are the Carnac, France, alignments, which include 2,935 menhirs. The alignments were probably used for ritual processions, and often a circle or semicircle of megaliths stood at one end.

The conception underlying the building of megalithic monuments is still unknown, but all of the monuments share certain architectural and technical features, demonstrating that the disseminators of the megalith idea came to dominate the local populations of many areas. The similarity of magical symbols carved on many of the monuments also shows an underlying unity of beliefs.

In most areas the megalith builders were superseded by the Beaker folk at the beginning of the Early Bronze Age. The newcomers, however, carried on the megalithic tradition by building round barrows for single burials, in contrast to the collective tombs of the Neolithic builders.

religious and astronomical purposes. Their layouts suggest a degree of mathematical sophistication that was first suspected only in the mid-20th century. Stonehenge is a circle, but some of the other megalithic structures are egg-shaped and, apparently, constructed on mathematical principles that require at least practical knowledge of the Pythagorean theorem that the square of the hypotenuse of a right triangle is equal to the sum of the squares of the other two sides. This theorem, or at least the Pythagorean numbers that can be generated by it, seems to have been known throughout Asia, the Middle East, and Neolithic Europe two millennia before the birth of Pythagoras.

The combination of religion and astronomy was fundamental to the early history of science. It is found in Mesopotamia, Egypt, China (although to a much lesser extent than elsewhere), Central America, and India. The spectacle of the heavens, with the clearly discernible order and regularity of most heavenly bodies highlighted by extraordinary events such as comets and novae and the peculiar motions of the planets, obviously was an irresistible intellectual puzzle to early mankind. In its search for order and regularity, the human mind could do no better than to seize upon the heavens as the paradigm of certain knowledge. Astronomy was to remain the queen of the sciences (welded solidly to theology) for the next 4,000 years.

Science, in its mature form, developed only in the West. But it is instructive to survey the protoscience that appeared in other areas, especially in light of the fact that until quite recently this knowledge was often, as in China, far superior to Western science.

# CHINA

As has already been noted, astronomy seems everywhere to have been the first science to emerge. Its intimate relation to religion gave it a ritual dimension that then stimulated the growth of mathematics. Chinese savants, for example, early devised a calendar and methods of plotting the

*A solar eclipse, February 1988.* Space Frontiers/Archive Photos/Getty Images

positions of stellar constellations. Since changes in the heavens presaged important changes on Earth (for the Chinese considered the universe to be a vast organism in which all elements were connected), astronomy and astrology were incorporated into the system of government from the very dawn of the Chinese state in the 2nd millennium BCE. As the Chinese bureaucracy developed, an accurate calendar became absolutely necessary to the maintenance of legitimacy and order. The result was a system of astronomical observations and records unparalleled elsewhere, thanks to which there are, today, star catalogs and observations of eclipses and novae that go back for millennia.

In other sciences, too, the overriding emphasis was on practicality, for the Chinese, almost alone among ancient peoples, did not fill the cosmos with gods and demons whose arbitrary wills determined events. Order was inherent and, therefore, expected. It was for man to detect and describe this order and to profit from it. Chemistry (or, rather, alchemy), medicine, geology, geography, and technology were all encouraged by the state and flourished. Practical knowledge of a high order permitted the Chinese to deal with practical problems for centuries on a level not attained in the West until the Renaissance.

# INDIA

Astronomy was studied in India for calendrical purposes to set the times for both practical and religious tasks. Primary emphasis was placed on solar and lunar motions, the fixed stars serving as a background against which these luminaries moved. Indian mathematics seems to have been quite advanced, with particular sophistication in geometrical and algebraic techniques. This latter branch was undoubtedly stimulated by the flexibility of the Indian system of numeration that later was to come into the West as the Hindu-Arabic numerals.

# AMERICA

Quite independently of China, India, and the other civilizations of Europe and Asia, the Maya of Central America, building upon older cultures, created a complex society in which astronomy and astrology played important roles. Determination of the calendar, again, had both practical and religious significance. Solar and lunar eclipses were important, as was the position of the bright planet Venus. No sophisticated mathematics are known to have been associated with this astronomy, but the Mayan calendar was both ingenious and the result of careful observation.

# MAYAN CALENDAR

The Mayan calendar is a dating system of the ancient Mayan civilization and the basis for all other calendars used by Mesoamerican civilizations. The calendar was based on a ritual cycle of 260 named days and a year of 365 days. Taken together, they form a longer cycle of 18,980 days, or 52 years of 365 days, called a "Calendar Round."

The original name of the 260-day cycle is unknown; it is variously referred to as the Tzolkin ("Count of Days"), divinatory calendar, ritual calendar, or simply the day calendar. Within the Tzolkin are two smaller cycles of days numbered from 1 to 13 and an ordered series of 20 named days. Although the names for the ritual days differed throughout Mesoamerica, scholars believe that the various calendars were synchronized based on their use in divination. In particular, each named day was thought to have certain fateful characteristics, but most of the details have been lost. Although the ritual day series was synchronized throughout Mesoamerica, the start of the 365-day year varied. The 365-day year was divided into 18 named months (*uinals*) of 20 days plus one month of 5 "nameless" days, called Uayeb. The nameless days were considered extremely unlucky, causing the Maya to observe them with fasting and sacrifices to deities. Each ordinary day had a fourfold designation—in order, day number and day name in the 260-day cycle and day number within the month and month name in the 365-day cycle. Thus, each of the 18,980 days in the Calendar Round had a unique designation (e.g., 12 Caban 15 Ceh).

The Maya erected stelae—i.e., stone slabs or pillars—on which they carved representative figures and important dates and events in their rulers' lives. To describe a given date more accurately, the Maya instituted the "Long Count," a continuous marking of time from a base date. Most historians think that 4 Ahau 8 Cumku (most likely August 11, 3114 BCE) was the base date used by the Maya for the start of the "Long Count" and the first "Great Cycle," a period of 5,125 years that ended on December 21, 2012 CE.

*Detail of a Mayan calendar, a dating system of the ancient Mayan civilization and the basis for all other calendars used by Mesoamerican civilizations.* **Michel de Leeuw/E+/ Getty Images**

# THE MIDDLE EAST

In the cradles of Western civilization in Egypt and Mesopotamia, there were two rather different situations. In Egypt there was an assumption of cosmic order guaranteed by a host of benevolent gods. But unlike China, whose rugged geography often produced disastrous floods, earthquakes, and violent storms that destroyed crops, Egypt was surpassingly placid and delightful. Egyptians found it difficult to believe that all ended with death; enormous intellectual and physical labour, therefore, was devoted to preserving life after death. Both Egyptian theology and the pyramids are testaments to this preoccupation. All of the important questions were answered by religion, so the Egyptians did not concern themselves overmuch with speculations about the universe. The stars and the planets had astrological significance in that the major heavenly bodies were assumed to "rule" the land when they were in the ascendant (from the succession of these "rules" came the seven-day week, after the five planets and the Sun and the Moon), but astronomy was largely limited to the calendrical calculations necessary to predict the annual life-giving flood of the Nile. None of this required much mathematics, and there was, consequently, little of any importance.

Mesopotamia was more like China. The life of the land depended upon the two great rivers, the Tigris and the Euphrates, as that of China depended upon the Huang Ho (Yellow River) and the Yangtze. The land was harsh and made habitable only by extensive damming and irrigation works. Storms, insects, floods, and invaders made life insecure. To create a stable society required both great technological skill, for the creation of hydraulic works, and the ability to hold off the forces of disruption. These latter were early identified with powerful and arbitrary gods who dominated Mesopotamian theology. The cities of the plain were centred on temples run by a priestly caste whose functions included the planning of major public works, such as canals, dams, and irrigation systems, the allocation of the resources of the city to its members, and the averting of a divine wrath that could wipe out everything.

Mathematics and astronomy thrived under these conditions. The number system, probably drawn from the system of weights and coinage, was based on 60 (it was in ancient Mesopotamia that the system of degrees, minutes, and seconds developed) and was adapted to a practical arithmetic. The heavens were the abode of the gods, and because heavenly phenomena were thought to presage terrestrial disasters, they were carefully observed and recorded. Out of these practices grew, first, a highly developed mathematics that went far beyond the requirements of daily business, and then, some centuries later, a descriptive astronomy that was the most sophisticated of the ancient world until the Greeks took it over and perfected it.

Nothing is known of the motives of these early mathematicians for carrying their studies beyond the calculations of volumes of dirt to be removed from canals and the provisions necessary for work parties. It may have been simply intellectual play—the role of playfulness in the history of science should not be underestimated—that led them onward to abstract algebra. There are texts from about 1700 BCE that are remarkable for their mathematical suppleness. Babylonian mathematicians knew the Pythagorean relationship well and used it constantly. They could solve simple quadratic equations and could even solve problems in compound interest involving exponents. From about a millennium later there are texts that utilize these skills to provide a very elaborate mathematical description of astronomical phenomena.

Although China and Mesopotamia provide examples of exact observation and precise description of nature, what is missing is explanation in the scientific mode. The Chinese assumed a cosmic order that was vaguely founded

*The yin and yang symbol suggests the two opposite principles or forces that make up all the aspects of life.*
Rattanapatphoto/Shutterstock.com

on the balance of opposite forces (yin-yang) and the harmony of the five elements (water, wood, metal, fire, and earth). Why this harmony obtained was not discussed. Similarly, the Egyptians found the world harmonious because the gods willed it so. For Babylonians and other Mesopotamian cultures, order existed only so long as all-powerful and capricious gods supported it. In all these societies, humans could describe nature and use it, but to understand it was the function of religion and magic, not reason. It was the Greeks who first sought to go beyond description and to arrive at reasonable explanations of natural phenomena that did not involve the arbitrary will of the gods. Gods might still play a role, as indeed they did for centuries to come, but even the gods were subject to rational laws.

# GREEK SCIENCE

There seems to be no good reason why the Hellenes, clustered in isolated city-states in a relatively poor and backward land, should have struck out into intellectual regions that were only dimly perceived, if at all, by the splendid civilizations of the Yangtze, the Tigris and Euphrates, and the Nile valleys. There were many differences between ancient Greece and the other civilizations, but perhaps the most significant was religion. What is striking about Greek religion, in contrast to the religions of Mesopotamia and Egypt, is its puerility. Both of the great river civilizations evolved complex theologies that served to answer most, if not all, of the large questions about mankind's place and destiny. Greek religion did not. It was, in fact, little more than a collection of folk tales, more appropriate to the campfire than to the temple. Perhaps this phenomenon was the result of the collapse of an earlier Greek civilization, now called Mycenaean, toward the end of the 2nd millennium BCE, when a dark age descended upon Greece that lasted for three centuries. All that was preserved were stories of gods and men, passed along by poets, that dimly reflected Mycenaean values and events. Such were the great poems of Homer, the *Iliad* and the *Odyssey*, in which heroes and gods mingled freely with one another. Indeed, they mingled too freely, for the gods appear in these tales as little more than immortal adolescents whose tricks and feats, when compared with the concerns of a Marduk or Jehovah, are infantile. There really was no Greek theology in the sense that theology provides a coherent and profound explanation of the workings of both the cosmos and the human heart. Hence, there were no easy answers to inquiring Greek minds. The result was that ample room was left for a more penetrating and ultimately more satisfying mode of inquiry. Thus were philosophy and its oldest offspring, science, born.

## THE BIRTH OF NATURAL PHILOSOPHY

The first natural philosopher, according to Hellenic tradition, was Thales of Miletus, who flourished in the 6th century BCE. We know of him only through later accounts, for nothing he wrote has survived. He is supposed to have predicted a solar eclipse in 585 BCE and to have invented the formal study of geometry in his demonstration of the bisecting of a circle by its diameter. Most importantly, he tried to explain all observed natural phenomena in terms of the changes of a single substance, water, which can be seen to exist in solid, liquid, and gaseous states. What for Thales guaranteed the regularity and rationality of the world was the innate divinity in all things that directed them to their divinely appointed ends. From these ideas there emerged two characteristics of classical Greek science. The first was the view of the universe as an ordered structure (the Greek *kósmos* means "order"). The second was the conviction that this order was not that of a mechanical contrivance but that of an organism; all parts of the universe had purposes in the overall scheme of things, and objects moved naturally toward the ends they were fated to serve. This motion toward ends is called teleology and, with but few exceptions, it permeated Greek as well as much later science

Thales inadvertently made one other fundamental contribution to the development of natural science. By naming a specific substance as the basic element of all matter, Thales opened himself to criticism, which was not long in coming. His own disciple, Anaximander, was quick to argue that water could not be the basic substance. His argument was simple: water, if it is anything, is essentially wet; nothing can be its own contradiction. Hence, if Thales were correct, the opposite of wet could not exist in a substance, and that would preclude all of the dry things that are observed in the world. Therefore, Thales was wrong. Here was the birth of the critical tradition that is fundamental to the advance of science.

Thales' conjectures set off an intellectual explosion, most of which was devoted to increasingly refined criticisms of his doctrine of fundamental matter. Various single substances were proposed and then rejected, ultimately in favour of a multiplicity of elements that could account for such opposite qualities as wet and dry, hot and cold. Two centuries after Thales, most natural philosophers accepted a doctrine of four elements: earth (cold and dry), fire (hot and dry), water (cold and wet), and air (hot and wet). All bodies were made from these four.

The presence of the elements only guaranteed the presence of their qualities in various proportions. What was not accounted for was the form these elements took, which served to differentiate natural objects from one another. The problem of form was first attacked systematically by the philosopher and cult leader Pythagoras in the 6th century BCE. Legend has it that Pythagoras became convinced of the primacy of number when he realized that the musical notes produced by a monochord were in simple ratio to the length of the string. Qualities (tones) were reduced to quantities (numbers in integral ratios). Thus was born mathematical physics, for this discovery provided the essential bridge between the world of physical experience and that of numerical relationships. Number provided the answer to the question of the origin of forms and qualities.

## ARISTOTLE AND ARCHIMEDES

Hellenic science was built upon the foundations laid by Thales and Pythagoras. It reached its zenith in the works of Aristotle and Archimedes. Aristotle represents the first tradition, that of qualitative forms and teleology. He was, himself, a biologist whose observations of marine organisms were unsurpassed until the 19th century. Biology is essentially teleological—the parts of a living organism are understood in terms of what they do in and for the organism—and Aristotle's biological works provided the framework for the science until the time of Charles Darwin. In physics, teleology is not so obvious, and Aristotle had to impose it on the cosmos. From Plato, his teacher, he inherited the theological proposition that the heavenly bodies (stars and planets) are literally divine and, as such, perfect. They could, therefore, move only in perfect, eternal, unchanging motion, which, by Plato's definition, meant perfect circles. The Earth, being obviously not divine, and inert, was at the centre. From the

Earth to the sphere of the Moon, all things constantly changed, generating new forms and then decaying back into formlessness. Above the Moon the cosmos consisted of contiguous and concentric crystalline spheres moving on axes set at angles to one another (this accounted for the peculiar motions of the planets) and deriving their motion either from a fifth element that moved naturally in circles or from heavenly souls resident in the celestial bodies. The ultimate cause of all motion was a prime, or unmoved, mover (God) that stood outside the cosmos.

Aristotle was able to make a great deal of sense of observed nature by asking of any object or process: what is the material involved, what is its form and how did it get that form, and, most important of all, what is its purpose? What should be noted is that, for Aristotle, all activity that occurred spontaneously was natural. Hence, the proper means of investigation was observation. Experiment, that is, altering natural conditions in order to throw light on the hidden properties and activities of objects, was unnatural and could not, therefore, be expected to reveal the essence of things. Experiment was thus not essential to Greek science.

The problem of purpose did not arise in the areas in which Archimedes made his most important contributions. He was, first of all, a brilliant mathematician whose work on conic sections and on the area of the circle prepared the way for the later invention of the calculus. It was in mathematical physics, however, that he made his greatest contributions to science. His mathematical demonstration of the law of the lever was as exact as a Euclidean proof in geometry. Similarly, his work on hydrostatics introduced and developed the method whereby physical characteristics, in this case specific gravity, which Archimedes discovered, are given mathematical shape and then manipulated by mathematical methods to yield mathematical conclusions that can be translated back into physical terms.

In one major area the Aristotelian and the Archimedean approaches were forced into a rather inconvenient marriage. Astronomy was the dominant physical science throughout antiquity, but it had never been successfully reduced to a coherent system. The Platonic-Aristotelian astral religion required that planetary orbits be circles. But, particularly after the conquests of Alexander the Great had made the observations and mathematical methods of the Babylonians available to the Greeks, astronomers found it impossible to reconcile theory and observation. Astronomy then split into two parts: one was physical and accepted Aristotelian theory in accounting for heavenly motion; the other ignored causation and concentrated solely on the creation of a mathematical model that could be used for computing planetary positions. Ptolemy, in the 2nd century CE, carried the latter tradition to its highest point in antiquity in his *He mathematike syntaxis* ("The Mathematical Collection," better known under its Greek-Arabic title, *Almagest*).

## MEDICINE

The Greeks not only made substantial progress in understanding the cosmos but also went far beyond their predecessors in their knowledge of the human body. Pre-Greek medicine had been almost entirely confined to religion and ritual. Disease was considered the result of divine disfavour and human sin, to be dealt with by spells, prayers, and other propitiatory measures. In the 5th century BCE a revolutionary change came about that is associated with the name of Hippocrates. It was Hippocrates and his school who, influenced by the rise of natural philosophy, first insisted that disease was a natural,

*Hippocrates is represented in an undated bust in the Louvre in Paris, France.* Universal Images Group/Getty Images

not a supernatural, phenomenon. Even maladies as striking as epilepsy, whose seizures appeared to be divinely caused, were held to originate in natural causes within the body.

The height of medical science in antiquity was reached late in the Hellenistic period. Much work was done at the museum of Alexandria, a research institute set up under Greek influence in Egypt in the 3rd century BCE to sponsor learning in general. The heart and the vascular system were investigated, as were the nerves and the brain. The organs of the thoracic cavity were described, and attempts were made to discover their functions. It was on these researches, and on his own dissections of apes and pigs, that the last great physician of antiquity, Galen of Pergamum, based his physiology. It was, essentially, a tripartite system in which so-called spirits—natural, vital, and animal—passed respectively through the veins, the arteries, and the nerves to vitalize the body as a whole. Galen's attempts to correlate therapeutics with his physiology were not successful, and so medical practice remained eclectic and a matter of the physician's choice. Usually the optimal choice was that propounded by the Hippocratics, who relied primarily on simple, clean living and the ability of the body to heal itself.

## SCIENCE IN ROME AND CHRISTIANITY

The apogee of Greek science in the works of Archimedes and Euclid coincided with the rise of Roman power in the Mediterranean. The Romans were deeply impressed by Greek art, literature, philosophy, and science, and after their conquest of Greece many Greek intellectuals served as household slaves tutoring noble Roman children. The Romans were a practical people, however, and, while they contemplated the Greek intellectual achievement with awe, they also could not help but ask what good it had done the Greeks. Roman common sense was what kept Rome great; science and philosophy were either ignored or relegated to rather low status. Even such a Hellenophile as the statesman and orator Cicero used Greek thought more to buttress the old Roman ways than as a source of new ideas and viewpoints.

The spirit of independent research was quite foreign to the Roman mind, so scientific innovation ground to a halt. The scientific legacy of Greece was condensed and corrupted into Roman encyclopaedias whose major function was entertainment rather than enlightenment. Typical of this spirit was the 1st-century-AD aristocrat Pliny the Elder, whose *Natural History* was a multivolume collection of myths, odd tales of wondrous creatures, magic, and some science, all mixed together uncritically for the titillation of other aristocrats. Aristotle would have been embarrassed by it.

At its height Rome incorporated a host of peoples with different customs, languages, and religions within its empire. One religious sect that proved more significant than the rest was Christianity. Jesus and his kingdom were not of this world, but his disciples and their followers were. This world could not be ignored, even though concern with worldly things could be dangerous to the soul. So the early Christians approached the worldly wisdom of their time with ambivalence: on the one hand, the rhetoric and the arguments of ancient philosophy were snares and delusions that might mislead the simple and the unwary; on the other hand, the sophisticated and the educated of the empire could not be converted unless the Christian message was presented in the terms and rhetoric of the philosophical schools. Before they knew it, the early Christians were enmeshed in metaphysical arguments,

*Pliny the Elder.* **Hulton Archive/Getty Images**

some of which involved physics. What, for example, was the nature of Jesus, in purely physical terms? How was it possible that anybody could have two different essential natures, as was claimed for Jesus? Such questions revealed how important knowledge of the arguments of Greek thinkers on the nature of substance could be to those engaged in founding a new theology.

Ancient learning, then, did not die with the fall of Rome and the occupation of the Western Empire by tribes of Germanic barbarians. To be sure, the lamp of learning burned very feebly, but it did not go out. Monks in monasteries faithfully copied out classics of ancient thought and early Christianity and preserved them for posterity. Monasteries continued to teach the elements of ancient learning, for little beyond the elementary survived in the Latin West. In the East, the Byzantine Empire remained strong, and there the ancient traditions continued. There was little original work done in the millennium following the fall of Rome, but the ancient texts were preserved along with knowledge of the ancient Greek language. This was to be a precious reservoir of learning for the Latin West in later centuries.

# SCIENCE IN ISLAM

The torch of ancient learning passed first to one of the invading groups that helped bring down the Eastern Empire. In the 7th century the Arabs, inspired by their new religion, burst out of the Arabian peninsula and laid the foundations of an Islamic empire that eventually rivalled that of ancient Rome. To the Arabs, ancient science was a precious treasure. The Qur'an, the sacred book of Islam, particularly praised medicine as an art close to God. Astronomy and astrology were believed to be one way of glimpsing what God willed for mankind. Contact with Hindu mathematics and the requirements of astronomy stimulated the study of numbers and of geometry. The writings of the Hellenes were, therefore, eagerly sought and translated, and thus much of the science of antiquity passed into Islamic culture. Greek medicine, Greek astronomy and astrology, and Greek mathematics, together with the great philosophical works of Plato and, particularly, Aristotle, were assimilated in Islam by the end of the 9th century. Nor did the Arabs stop with assimilation. They criticized and they innovated. Islamic astronomy and astrology were aided by the construction of great astronomical observatories that provided accurate observations against which the Ptolemaic predictions could be checked. Numbers fascinated Islamic thinkers, and this fascination served as the motivation for the creation of algebra (from Arabic *al-jabr*) and the study of algebraic functions.

## MEDIEVAL EUROPEAN SCIENCE

Medieval Christendom confronted Islam chiefly in military crusades, in Spain and the Holy Land, and in theology. From this confrontation came the restoration of ancient learning to the West. The Reconquista in Spain gradually pushed the Moors south from the Pyrenees, and among the treasures left behind were Arabic translations of Greek works of science and philosophy. In 1085 the city of Toledo, with one of the finest libraries in Islam, fell to the Christians. Among the occupiers were Christian monks who quickly began the process of translating ancient works into Latin. By the end of the 12th century much of the ancient heritage was again available to the Latin West.

The medieval world was caricatured by thinkers of the 18th-century Enlightenment as a period of darkness, superstition, and hostility to science and learning. On the contrary, it was one of great technological vitality. The advances that were made may appear today as trifling, but that is because they were so fundamental. They included the horseshoe and the horse collar, without which horsepower cannot be efficiently exploited. The invention of the crank, the brace and bit, the wheelbarrow, and the

*A traditional Dutch windmill in the Netherlands.* Peter Kirillov/ Shutterstock.com

*The Notre-Dame de Paris, France. It is the most famous of the Gothic cathedrals of the Middle Ages and is distinguished for its size, antiquity, and architectural interest. The half arches that are known as flying buttresses can be seen supporting the building.* Purestock/Thinkstock

flying buttress made possible the great Gothic cathedrals. Improvements in the gear trains of waterwheels and the development of windmills harnessed these sources of power with great efficiency. Mechanical ingenuity, building on experience with mills and power wheels, culminated in the 14th century in the mechanical clock, which not only set a new standard of chronometrical accuracy but also provided philosophers with a new metaphor for nature itself.

An equal amount of energy was devoted to achieving a scientific understanding of nature, but it is essential to understand to what use medieval thinkers put this kind of knowledge. As the fertility of the technology shows, medieval Europeans had no deep prejudices against utilitarian knowledge. But the areas in which scientific knowledge could find useful expression were few. Instead, science was viewed chiefly as a means of understanding God's creation and, thereby, the Godhead itself. The best example of this attitude is found in the medieval study of optics. Light, as Genesis makes clear, was among the first creations of God. The 12th-13th-century cleric-scholar Robert Grosseteste saw in light the first creative impulse. As light spread it created both space and matter, and, in its reflection from the outermost circle of the cosmos, it gradually solidified into the heavenly spheres. To understand the laws of the propagation of light was to understand, in some slight way, the nature of the creation.

In the course of studying light, particular problems were isolated and attacked. What, for example, is the rainbow? It is impossible to get close enough to a rainbow to see clearly what is going on, for as the observer moves, so too does the rainbow. It does seem to depend upon the presence of raindrops, so medieval investigators sought to bring the rainbow down from the skies into their studies. Insight into the nature of the rainbow could be achieved

*The sun shining from behind clouds.* **Matthew Bowden/Fotolia**

by simulating the conditions under which rainbows occur. For raindrops the investigators substituted hollow glass balls filled with water, so that the rainbow could be studied at leisure. Valid conclusions about rainbows could then be drawn by assuming the validity of the analogy between raindrops and water-filled globes. This involved the implicit assumptions that nature was simple (i.e., governed by a few general laws) and that similar effects had similar causes. Such a nature was what could be expected of a rational, benevolent deity; hence, the assumption could be persuasively adopted.

Medieval philosophers were not content, as the rainbow example shows, to repeat what the ancients had said. They subjected ancient texts to close critical scrutiny. Usually the intensity of the criticism was directly

# RAINBOWS

When light from a distant source, such as the Sun, strikes a collection of water drops—such as rain, spray, or fog—a rainbow may appear. It appears as a multicolored arc whose "ends" seem to touch the Earth. Rainbows are seen only when the observer is between the Sun and the water drops, so rainbows appear in the part of the sky opposite the sun. The centre of the rainbow's arc is located on an imaginary line extending from the light source through the observer's eye to the area of the water drops.

Rainbows are most commonly seen when the Sun's rays strike raindrops falling from distant rain clouds. Generally, this is only in the early morning or late afternoon. When the Sun is too far above the horizon no rainbow can be seen. When the Sun is lower in the sky, however, part of the arc becomes visible. In fact, if the Sun is low enough and the observer is located in

*Rainbow over an alpine pass in Switzerland.* K. Kolygo/ Shutterstock.com

a place that is high enough, such as on a mountain or in an airplane, the observer may see a circular rainbow.

The most brilliant and most commonly seen rainbow is called the primary rainbow. The arcs of color in a rainbow are caused by the refraction, or bending, and internal reflection of light rays that enter the raindrops. A ray of white sunlight is actually composed of all the colors of the spectrum. Inside the drop the ray of white light is separated into the colors that make it up and reflected back toward the observer. In the primary rainbow the colors are, from inside to outside, violet, blue, green, yellow, orange, and red. The red band makes an angle of about 42 degrees with the sun's rays, and the other colored bands make successively smaller angles. Sometimes another less intense rainbow may also be seen; this is called the secondary bow. The secondary bow, when visible, is seen outside the primary bow and with its color sequence reversed. It is produced by light that has been reflected from two different points on the back of the drop before emerging into the air. Higher-order rainbows are very weak and so are rarely seen.

Occasionally, faintly colored rings are seen just inside the primary bow. These are called spurious, or supernumerary, bows. When raindrops are extremely fine, an almost white bow, called a fogbow, is produced. A fogbow at night, sometimes called a lunar rainbow, is made by sunlight reflected from the Moon and appears as a ring around the Moon.

proportional to the theological significance of the problem involved. Such was the case with motion. Medieval philosophers examined all aspects of motion with great care, for the nature of motion had important theological implications. Thomas Aquinas used Aristotle's dictum, that everything that moves is moved by something else, to show that God must exist, for otherwise the existence of any motion would imply an infinite regression of prior causal motions.

It should be clear that there was no conscious conflict between science and religion in the Middle Ages. As Aquinas pointed out, God was the author of both the book of Scripture and the book of nature. The guide to nature was reason, the faculty that was the image of God in which mankind was made. Scripture was direct revelation, although it needed interpretation, for there were passages that were obscure or difficult. The two books, having the same author, could not contradict each other. For the short term, science and revelation marched hand in hand. Aquinas carefully wove knowledge of nature into his theology, as in his proof from motion of the existence of God. But if his scientific concepts of motion should ever be challenged, there would necessarily be a theological challenge as well. By working science into the very fabric of his theology, he virtually guaranteed that someday there would be conflict. Theologians would side with theology and scientists with science, to create a breach that neither particularly desired.

The glory of medieval science was its integration of science, philosophy, and theology into a magnificent and comprehensible whole. It can be best contemplated in the greatest of all medieval poems, *The Divine Comedy* by the Italian writer, poet, literary theorist, moral philosopher, and political thinker Dante Alighieri. Here Dante had created an essentially Aristotelian cosmos, finite and easily understood, over which God, his Son, and his saints reigned. Humanity and the Earth occupied the centre, as befitted their centrality in God's plan. The nine circles of hell were populated by humans whose exercise of their free will had led to their damnation. Purgatory contained lesser sinners still capable of salvation. The heavenly spheres were populated by the saved and the saintly. The natural hierarchy gave way to the spiritual hierarchy as one ascended toward the throne of God. Such a hierarchy was reflected in the social and political institutions of medieval Europe, and God, the supreme monarch, ruled his creation with justice and love. All fit together in a grand cosmic scheme, one not to be abandoned lightly.

# THE RISE OF
# MODERN SCIENCE

E ven as Dante was writing his great work, deep forces were threatening the unitary cosmos he celebrated. The pace of technological innovation began to quicken. Particularly in Italy, the political demands of the time gave new importance to technology, and a new profession emerged, that of civil and military engineer. These people faced practical problems that demanded practical solutions. Leonardo da Vinci is certainly the most famous of them, though he was much more as well. A painter of genius, he closely studied human anatomy in order to give verisimilitude to his paintings. As a sculptor he mastered the difficult techniques of casting metal. As a producer-director of the form of Renaissance dramatic production called the masque, he devised complicated machinery to create special effects. But it was as a military engineer that he observed the path of a mortar bomb being lobbed over a city wall and insisted that the projectile did not follow two straight lines—a slanted ascent followed by a vertical drop—as Aristotle had said it must. Leonardo and his colleagues needed to know nature truly; no amount of book learning could substitute for actual experience, nor could books impose their authority upon phenomena. What

Aristotle and his commentators asserted as philosophical necessity often did not gibe with what could be seen with one's own eyes. The hold of ancient philosophy was too strong to be broken lightly, but a healthy skepticism began to emerge.

# THE AUTHORITY OF PHENOMENA

The first really serious blow to the traditional acceptance of ancient authorities was the discovery of the New World at the end of the 15th century. Ptolemy, the great astronomer and geographer, had insisted that only the three continents of Europe, Africa, and Asia could exist, and Christian scholars from St. Augustine on had accepted it, for otherwise men would have to walk upside down at the antipodes. But Ptolemy, St. Augustine, and a host of other authorities were wrong. The dramatic expansion of the known world also served to stimulate the study of mathematics, for wealth and fame awaited those who could turn navigation into a real and trustworthy science.

In large part the Renaissance was a time of feverish intellectual activity devoted to the complete recovery of the ancient heritage. To the Aristotelian texts that had been the foundation of medieval thought were added translations of Plato, with his vision of mathematical harmonies, of Galen, with his experiments in physiology and anatomy, and, perhaps most important of all, of Archimedes, who showed how theoretical physics could be done outside the traditional philosophical framework. The results were subversive.

The search for antiquity turned up a peculiar bundle of manuscripts that added a decisive impulse to the direction in which Renaissance science was moving.

*Hermes Trismegistos.* National Library of Medicine

These manuscripts were taken to have been written by or to report almost at first hand the activities of the legendary priest, prophet, and sage Hermes Trismegistos. Hermes was supposedly a contemporary of Moses, and the Hermetic writings contained an alternative story of creation that gave man a far more prominent role than the traditional account. God had made man fully in his image: a creator, not just a rational animal. Man could imitate God by creating. To do so, he must learn nature's secrets, and this could be done only by forcing nature to yield them through the tortures of fire, distillation, and other alchemical manipulations. The reward for success would be eternal life and youth, as well as freedom from want and disease. It was a heady vision, and it gave rise to the notion that, through science and technology, man could bend nature to his wishes. This is essentially the modern view of science, and it should be emphasized that it occurs only in Western civilization. It is probably this attitude that permitted the West to surpass the East, after centuries of inferiority, in the exploitation of the physical world.

# THE SCIENTIFIC REVOLUTION

The Hermetic tradition also had more specific effects. Inspired, as is now known, by late Platonist mysticism, the Hermetic writers had rhapsodized on enlightenment and on the source of light, the Sun. Marsilio Ficino, the 15th-century Florentine translator of both Plato and the Hermetic writings, composed a treatise on the Sun that came close to idolatry. A young Polish student visiting Italy at the turn of the 16th century was touched by this current. Back in Poland, he began to work on the problems posed by the Ptolemaic astronomical system. With the blessing of the church, which he served formally as a canon, Nicolaus Copernicus set out to modernize the astronomical apparatus by which the church made such important calculations as the proper dates for Easter and other festivals.

## COPERNICUS

In 1543, as he lay on his deathbed, Copernicus finished reading the proofs of his great work; he died just as it was published. His *De revolutionibus orbium coelestium libri VI* ("Six Books Concerning the Revolutions of the Heavenly Orbs") was the opening shot in a revolution whose consequences were greater than those of any other intellectual event in the history of mankind. The scientific revolution radically altered the conditions of thought and of material existence in which the human race lives, and its effects are not yet exhausted.

All this was caused by Copernicus's daring in placing the Sun, not the Earth, at the centre of the cosmos. Copernicus actually cited Hermes Trismegistos to justify this idea, and his language was thoroughly Platonic. But he meant his work as a serious work in astronomy, not philosophy, so he set out to justify it observationally and mathematically. The results were impressive. At one stroke, Copernicus reduced a complexity verging on chaos to elegant simplicity. The apparent back-and-forth movements of the planets, which required prodigious ingenuity to accommodate within the Ptolemaic system, could be accounted for just in terms of the Earth's own orbital motion added to or subtracted from the motions of the planets. Variation in planetary brightness was also explained by this combination of motions. The fact that Mercury and Venus were never found opposite the Sun in the sky Copernicus explained by placing their orbits closer to the Sun than that of the Earth. Indeed, Copernicus was able to place the planets in order of their distances from the Sun by considering their speeds and thus to construct a system of the planets, something that had eluded Ptolemy. This system had a simplicity, coherence, and aesthetic charm that made it irresistible

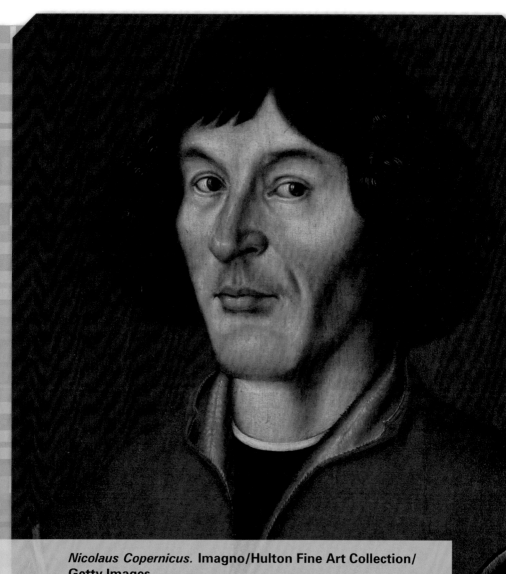

*Nicolaus Copernicus.* **Imagno/Hulton Fine Art Collection/ Getty Images**

# COPERNICAN SYSTEM

In astronomy, the model of the solar system centred on the Sun, with Earth and other planets moving around it, formulated by Nicolaus Copernicus, and published in 1543 is known as the Copernican system. It appeared with an introduction by Rhäticus (Rheticus) in the previously mentioned *De revolutionibus orbium coelestium libri VI*. The Copernican system gave a truer picture than the older Ptolemaic system, which was geocentric, or centred on Earth. The Copernican system correctly described the Sun as having a central position relative to Earth and other planets. Copernicus retained from Ptolemy of Alexandria, although in somewhat altered form, the imaginary clockwork of epicycles and deferents (orbital circles upon circles), to explain the seemingly irregular movements of the planets in terms of circular motion at uniform speeds.

to those who felt that God was the supreme artist. His was not a rigorous argument, but aesthetic considerations are not to be ignored in the history of science.

Copernicus did not solve all of the difficulties of the Ptolemaic system. He had to keep some of the cumbrous apparatus of epicycles and other geometrical adjustments, as well as a few Aristotelian crystalline spheres. The result was neater, but not so striking that it commanded immediate universal assent. Moreover, there were some implications that caused considerable concern: Why should the crystalline orb containing the Earth circle the Sun? And how was it possible for the Earth itself to revolve on its axis once in 24 hours without hurling all objects, including humans, off its surface? No known physics could answer these questions, and the provision of such answers was to be the central concern of the scientific revolution.

More was at stake than physics and astronomy, for one of the implications of the Copernican system struck at the very foundations of contemporary society. If the Earth revolved around the Sun, then the apparent positions of the fixed stars should shift as the Earth moves in its orbit. Copernicus and his contemporaries could detect no such shift (called stellar parallax), and there were only two interpretations possible to explain this failure. Either the Earth was at the centre, in which case no parallax was to be expected, or the stars were so far away that the parallax was too small to be detected. Copernicus chose the latter and thereby had to accept an enormous cosmos consisting mostly of empty space. God, it had been assumed, did nothing in vain, so for what purposes might he have created a universe in which the Earth and mankind were lost in immense space? To accept Copernicus was to give up the Dantean cosmos. The Aristotelian hierarchy of social place, political position, and theological gradation would vanish, to be replaced by the flatness and plainness of Euclidean space. It was a grim prospect and not one that recommended itself to most 16th-century intellectuals, and so Copernicus's grand idea remained on the periphery of astronomical thought. All astronomers were aware of it, some measured their own views against it, but only a small handful eagerly accepted it.

In the century and a half following Copernicus, two easily discernible scientific movements developed. The first was critical, the second, innovative and synthetic. They worked together to bring the old cosmos into disrepute and, ultimately, to replace it with a new one. Although they existed side by side, their effects can more easily be seen if they are treated separately.

## TYCHO, KEPLER, AND GALILEO

The critical tradition began with Copernicus. It led directly to the work of Tycho Brahe, who measured stellar and planetary positions more accurately than had anyone

*Tycho Brahe.* **Photos.com/Thinkstock**

before him. But measurement alone could not decide between Copernicus and Ptolemy, and Tycho insisted that the Earth was motionless. Copernicus did persuade Tycho to move the centre of revolution of all other planets to the Sun. To do so, he had to abandon the Aristotelian crystalline spheres that otherwise would collide with one another. Tycho also cast doubt upon the Aristotelian doctrine of heavenly perfection, for when, in the 1570s, a comet and a new star appeared, Tycho showed that they were both above the sphere of the Moon. Perhaps the most serious critical blows struck were those delivered by Galileo after the invention of the telescope. In quick succession, he announced that there were mountains on the Moon, satellites circling Jupiter, and spots upon the Sun. Moreover, the Milky Way was composed of countless stars whose existence no one had suspected until Galileo saw them. Here was criticism that struck at the very roots of Aristotle's system of the world.

At the same time Galileo was searching the heavens with his telescope, in Germany Johannes Kepler was searching them with his mind. Tycho's precise observations permitted Kepler to discover that Mars (and, by analogy, all the other planets) did not revolve in a circle at all, but in an ellipse, with the Sun at one focus. Ellipses tied all the planets together in grand Copernican harmony. The Keplerian cosmos was most un-Aristotelian, but Kepler hid his discoveries by burying them in almost impenetrable Latin prose in a series of works that did not circulate widely.

What Galileo and Kepler could not provide, although they tried, was an alternative to Aristotle that made equal sense. If the Earth revolves on its axis, then why do objects not fly off it? And why do objects dropped from towers not fall to the west as the Earth rotates to the east beneath them? And how is it possible for the Earth, suspended in

*Johannes Kepler.* Universal Images Group/Getty Images

empty space, to go around the Sun—whether in circles or ellipses—without anything pushing it? The answers were long in coming.

Galileo attacked the problems of the Earth's rotation and its revolution by logical analysis. Bodies do not fly off the Earth because they are not really revolving rapidly, even though their speed is high. In revolutions per minute, any body on the Earth is going very slowly and, therefore,

*Galileo.* **Universal Images Group/Getty Images**

has little tendency to fly off. Bodies fall to the base of towers from which they are dropped because they share with the tower the rotation of the Earth. Hence, bodies already in motion preserve that motion when another motion is added. So, Galileo deduced, a ball dropped from the top of a mast of a moving ship would fall at the base of the mast. If the ball were allowed to move on a frictionless horizontal plane, it would continue to move forever. Hence, Galileo concluded, the planets, once set in circular motion, continue to move in circles forever. Therefore, Copernican orbits exist. Galileo never acknowledged Kepler's ellipses; to do so would have meant abandoning his solution to the Copernican problem.

Kepler realized that there was a real problem with planetary motion. He sought to solve it by appealing to the one force that appeared to be cosmic in nature, namely magnetism. The Earth had been shown to be a giant magnet by William Gilbert in 1600, and Kepler seized upon this fact. A magnetic force, Kepler argued, emanated from the Sun and pushed the planets around in their orbits, but he was never able to quantify this rather vague and unsatisfactory idea.

By the end of the first quarter of the 17th century Aristotelianism was rapidly dying, but there was no satisfactory system to take its place. The result was a mood of skepticism and unease, for, as one observer put it, "The new philosophy calls all in doubt." It was this void that accounted largely for the success of a rather crude system proposed by René Descartes. Matter and motion were taken by Descartes to explain everything by means of mechanical models of natural processes, even though he warned that such models were not the way nature probably worked. They provided merely "likely stories," which seemed better than no explanation at all.

Armed with matter and motion, Descartes attacked the basic Copernican problems. Bodies once in motion, Descartes argued, remain in motion in a straight line unless and until they are deflected from this line by the impact of another body. All changes of motion are the result of such impacts. Hence, the ball falls at the foot of the mast because, unless struck by another body, it continues to move with the ship. Planets move around the Sun because they are swept around by whirlpools of a subtle matter filling all space. Similar models could be constructed to account for all phenomena; the Aristotelian system could be replaced by the Cartesian. There was one major problem, however, and it sufficed to bring down Cartesianism. Cartesian matter and motion had no purpose, nor did Descartes's philosophy seem to need the active participation of a deity. The Cartesian cosmos, as Voltaire later put it, was like a watch that had been wound up at the creation and continues ticking to eternity.

# NEWTON

The 17th century was a time of zealous religious feeling, and nowhere was that feeling more intense than in Great Britain. There a devout young man, Isaac Newton, was finally to discover the way to a new synthesis in which truth was revealed and God was preserved.

Newton was both an experimental and a mathematical genius, a combination that enabled him to establish both the Copernican system and a new mechanics. His method was simplicity itself: "from the phenomena of motions to investigate the forces of nature, and then from these forces to demonstrate the other phenomena." Newton's genius guided him in the selection of phenomena to be investigated, and his creation of a fundamental mathematical tool—the calculus (simultaneously invented by Gottfried

# PHILOSOPHIÆ
## NATURALIS
# PRINCIPIA
## MATHEMATICA.

Autore *JS. NEWTON*, *Trin. Coll. Cantab. Soc.* Matheseos Professore *Lucasiano*, & Societatis Regalis Sodali.

## IMPRIMATUR·
### S. P E P Y S, *Reg. Soc.* P R Æ S E S.
*Julii* 5. 1686.

### L O N D I N I,
Jussu *Societatis Regiæ* ac Typis *Josephi Streater*
les apud *Sam. Smith* ad insignia Principis *Wa*
D. *Pauli*, aliosq; nonnullos Bibliopolas. *Anno*

*Isaac Newton and the title page
from his De Philosophiae Naturalis
Principia Mathematica (1687;
Mathematical Principles of Natural
Philosophy).* **Science & Society
Picture Library/Getty Images**

Leibniz)—permitted him to submit the forces he inferred to calculation. The result was *Philosophiae Naturalis Principia Mathematica* (*Mathematical Principles of Natural Philosophy*, usually called simply the *Principia*), which appeared in 1687. Here was a new physics that applied equally well to terrestrial and celestial bodies. Copernicus, Kepler, and Galileo were all justified by Newton's analysis of forces. Descartes was utterly routed.

Newton's three laws of motion and his principle of universal gravitation sufficed to regulate the new cosmos, but only, Newton believed, with the help of God. Gravity, he more than once hinted, was direct divine action, as were all forces for order and vitality. Absolute space, for Newton, was essential, because space was the "sensorium of God," and the divine abode must necessarily be the ultimate coordinate system. Finally, Newton's analysis of the mutual perturbations of the planets caused by their individual gravitational fields predicted the natural collapse of the solar system unless God acted to set things right again.

## THE DIFFUSION OF SCIENTIFIC METHOD

The publication of the *Principia* marks the culmination of the movement begun by Copernicus and, as such, has always stood as the symbol of the scientific revolution. There were, however, similar attempts to criticize, systematize, and organize natural knowledge that did not lead to such dramatic results. In the same year as Copernicus's great volume, there appeared an equally important book on anatomy: Andreas Vesalius's *De humani corporis fabrica* ("On the Fabric of the Human Body," called the *De fabrica*), a critical examination of Galen's anatomy in which Vesalius drew on his own studies to correct many of Galen's errors. Vesalius, like Newton a century later, emphasized the phenomena, i.e., the accurate description

*Students at St. John's College replicating William Harvey's 17th-century dissection of an ox heart, c. 1940.* Alfred Eisenstaedt/Time & Life Pictures/Getty Images

of natural facts. Vesalius's work touched off a flurry of anatomical work in Italy and elsewhere that culminated in the discovery of the circulation of the blood by William Harvey, whose *Exercitatio Anatomica De Motu Cordis et Sanguinis in Animalibus* (*An Anatomical Exercise Concerning the Motion of the Heart and Blood in Animals*) was published in 1628. This was the *Principia* of physiology that established anatomy and physiology as sciences in their own right. Harvey showed that organic phenomena could be studied experimentally and that some organic processes could be reduced to mechanical systems. The heart and the vascular system could be considered as a pump and a system of pipes and could be understood without recourse to spirits or other forces immune to analysis.

In other sciences the attempt to systematize and criticize was not so successful. In chemistry, for example, the work of the medieval and early modern alchemists had yielded important new substances and processes, such as the mineral acids and distillation, but had obscured theory in almost impenetrable mystical argot. Robert Boyle in England tried to clear away some of the intellectual underbrush by insisting upon clear descriptions, reproducibility of experiments, and mechanical conceptions of chemical processes. Chemistry, however, was not yet ripe for revolution.

In many areas there was little hope of reducing phenomena to comprehensibility, simply because of the sheer number of facts to be accounted for. New instruments such as the microscope and the telescope vastly multiplied the worlds with which man had to reckon. The voyages of discovery brought back a flood of new botanical and zoological specimens that overwhelmed ancient classificatory schemes. The best that could be done was to describe new things accurately and hope that someday they could all be fitted together in a coherent way.

The growing flood of information put heavy strains upon old institutions and practices. It was no longer sufficient to publish scientific results in an expensive book that few could buy; information had to be spread widely and rapidly. Nor could the isolated genius, such as Newton, comprehend a world in which new information was being produced faster than any single person could assimilate it. Natural philosophers had to be sure of their data, and to that end they required independent and critical confirmation of their discoveries. New means were created to accomplish these ends.

Scientific societies sprang up, beginning in Italy in the early years of the 17th century and culminating in the two great national scientific societies that mark the zenith of the scientific revolution: the Royal Society of London for the Promotion of Natural Knowledge, created by royal charter in 1662, and the Académie des Sciences of Paris, formed in 1666. In these societies and others like them all over the world, natural philosophers could gather to examine, discuss, and criticize new discoveries and old theories. To provide a firm basis for these discussions, societies began to publish scientific papers. The Royal Society's *Philosophical Transactions*, which began as a private venture of its secretary, was the first such professional scientific journal. It was soon copied by the French academy's *Mémoires*, which won equal importance and prestige. The old practice of hiding new discoveries in private jargon, obscure language, or even anagrams gradually gave way to the ideal of universal comprehensibility. New canons of reporting were devised so that experiments and discoveries could be reproduced by others. This required new precision in language and a willingness to share experimental or observational methods. The failure of others to reproduce results cast serious doubts upon the original reports. Thus were created the tools for a massive assault on nature's secrets.

# ACADÉMIE DES SCIENCES

The French Académie des Sciences was established in Paris in 1666 under the patronage of Louis XIV to advise the French government on scientific matters. This advisory role has been largely taken over by other bodies, but the academy is still an important representative of French science on the international stage. Although its role is now predominantly honorific, the academy continues to hold regular Monday meetings at the Institut de France in Paris.

The Academy of Sciences was established by Louis's financial controller, Jean-Baptiste Colbert, to formalize under government control earlier private meetings on scientific matters. In 1699 the academy received a formal constitution, in which six subject areas were recognized: mathematics, mechanics, astronomy, chemistry, botany, and anatomy. There was a hierarchy of membership, in which the senior members (known as pensioners, who received a small remuneration) were followed by associates and assistants.

The academy organized several important expeditions. For example, in 1736 Pierre-Louis Moreau de Maupertuis led an expedition to Lapland to measure the length of a degree along the meridian. His measurement verified Isaac Newton's contention that the Earth is an oblate spheroid (a sphere flattened at the poles).

Following the French Revolution of 1789, the academy was directed in 1791 by the National Assembly to rationalize the nation's system of weights and measures; this resulted in the adoption of the metric system. In 1793, during a period of revolutionary egalitarianism, the academy was temporarily abolished, together with other royal academies, because of its royalist title and elitist nature. In 1795 the academy was revived under the title of First Class of the National Institute. The idea of the institute was to combine under one organization the main formerly separate royal academies, which together represented all branches of learning and culture. Science, however, was placed first according to the ideology of the Enlightenment and was the largest group. At the Bourbon Restoration of Louis XVIII in 1816, the academy resumed its former title, though it remains a constituent section of the National Institute, which now includes the French Academy; the Academy of Fine Arts; the Academy of Inscriptions and Belles-Lettres; and the Academy of Moral and Political Sciences.

In 1835 the academy began publication of its *Comptes rendus*, a weekly journal of its proceedings that appeared within the week, thus creating a precedent for the rapid publication of scientific news. The *Comptes* largely superseded the annual volume of *Mémoires*, and it is still the academy's principal publication. The academy has a limited government budget and is officially answerable to the minister of education. In the 19th century, the academy wielded great power through publication, prizes, and patronage for academic posts. Unlike the Royal Society of London, its (resident) membership was strictly limited (to 75 in the 1800s), and elections were hotly contested, voting being restricted to resident members. It was usual for candidates to stand several times before being successful. Marie Curie tried only once in 1910 and was narrowly defeated. Charles Darwin was nominated several times before finally being elected as a corresponding member in 1878. On the other hand, the academy could boast of its association with many eminent French scientists, such as Antoine-Laurent Lavoisier, Pierre-Simon Laplace, and Louis Pasteur.

Even with the scientific revolution accomplished, much remained to be done. Again, it was Newton who showed the way. For the macroscopic world, the *Principia* sufficed. Newton's three laws of motion and the principle of universal gravitation were all that was necessary to analyze the mechanical relations of ordinary bodies, and the calculus provided the essential mathematical tools. For the microscopic world, Newton provided two methods. Where simple laws of action had already been determined from observation, as the relation of volume and pressure of a gas (Boyle's law, $pv = k$), Newton assumed forces between particles that permitted him to derive the law. He then used these forces to predict other phenomena, in this case the speed of sound in air, that could be measured against the prediction. Conformity of observation to prediction was taken as evidence for the essential truth of the theory. Second, Newton's method made possible the discovery of laws of macroscopic action that could be accounted for by microscopic forces. Here the seminal work was not the *Principia* but Newton's masterpiece of experimental physics, the *Opticks*, published in 1704, in which he showed how to examine a subject experimentally and discover the laws concealed therein. Newton showed how judicious use of hypotheses could open the way to further experimental investigation until a coherent theory was achieved. The *Opticks* was to serve as the model in the 18th and early 19th centuries for the investigation of heat, light, electricity, magnetism, and chemical atoms.

# THE CLASSIC AGE OF SCIENCE

J ust as the *Principia* preceded the *Opticks*, so, too, did mechanics maintain its priority among the sciences in the 18th century, in the process becoming transformed from a branch of physics into a branch of mathematics. Many physical problems were reduced to mathematical ones that proved amenable to solution by increasingly sophisticated analytical methods. The Swiss mathematician and physicist Leonhard Euler was one of the most fertile and prolific workers in those two fields. His development of the calculus of variations provided a powerful tool for dealing with highly complex problems. In France, Jean Le Rond d'Alembert and Joseph-Louis Lagrange succeeded in completely mathematizing mechanics, reducing it to an axiomatic system requiring only mathematical manipulation.

## MECHANICS

The test of Newtonian mechanics was its congruence with physical reality. At the beginning of the 18th century it was put to a rigorous test. Cartesians insisted that the Earth, because it was squeezed at the Equator by the etherial vortex causing gravity, should be somewhat pointed at the poles, a shape rather like that of an American football; Newtonians, arguing that centrifugal force was greatest at the Equator, calculated an oblate sphere that was flattened at the poles and bulged at the Equator. The Newtonians were proved correct after careful measurements of a degree of the meridian were made on expeditions to Lapland and to Peru. The final touch to the Newtonian edifice was provided by Pierre-Simon, marquis de Laplace, whose masterly *Traité de mécanique céleste* (1798–1827; *Celestial Mechanics*) systematized everything that had been done in celestial mechanics under Newton's inspiration. Laplace went beyond Newton by showing that the perturbations of the planetary orbits caused by the interactions of planetary gravitation are in fact periodic and that the solar system is, therefore, stable, requiring no divine intervention.

# CHEMISTRY

Although Newton was unable to bring to chemistry the kind of clarification he brought to physics, the *Opticks* did provide a method for the study of chemical phenomena. One of the major advances in chemistry in the 18th century was the discovery of the role of air, and of gases generally, in chemical reactions. This role had been dimly glimpsed in the 17th century, but it was not fully seen until the classic experiments of Joseph Black on *magnesia alba* (basic magnesium carbonate) in the 1750s. By extensive and careful use of the chemical balance, Black showed that an air with specific properties could combine with solid substances such as quicklime and could be recovered from them. This discovery served to focus attention

*Antoine-Laurent Lavoisier.* Science Source/Photo
Researchers/Getty Images

on the properties of "air," which was soon found to be a generic, not a specific, name. Chemists discovered a host of specific gases and investigated their various properties: some were flammable, others put out flames; some killed animals, others made them lively. Clearly, gases had a great deal to do with chemistry.

The Newton of chemistry was Antoine-Laurent Lavoisier. In a series of carefully balanced experiments he untangled combustion reactions to show that, in contradiction to established theory, which held that a body gave off the principle of inflammation (called phlogiston) when it burned, combustion actually involves the combination of bodies with a gas that Lavoisier named oxygen. The chemical revolution was as much a revolution in method as in conception. Gravimetric methods made possible precise analysis, and this, Lavoisier insisted, was the central concern of the new chemistry. Only when bodies were analyzed as to their constituent substances was it possible to classify them and their attributes logically and consistently.

# THE IMPONDERABLE FLUIDS

The Newtonian method of inferring laws from close observation of phenomena and then deducing forces from these laws was applied with great success to phenomena in which no ponderable matter figured. Light, heat, electricity, and magnetism were all entities that were not capable of being weighed, i.e., imponderable. In the *Opticks*, Newton had assumed that particles of different sizes could account for the different refrangibility of the various colours of light. Clearly, forces of some sort must be associated with these particles if such phenomena as diffraction and refraction are to be accounted for. During the 18th century heat, electricity, and magnetism were similarly conceived as consisting of particles with which were associated forces of attraction or repulsion. In the 1780s, Charles-Augustin de Coulomb was able to measure electrical and magnetic forces, using a delicate torsion balance of his own invention, and to show that these forces follow the general form of Newtonian universal attraction. Only light and heat failed to disclose such general force laws, thereby resisting reduction to Newtonian mechanics.

# SCIENCE AND THE INDUSTRIAL REVOLUTION

It has long been a commonsensical notion that the rise of modern science and the Industrial Revolution were closely connected. It is difficult to show any direct effect of scientific discoveries upon the rise of the textile or even the metallurgical industry in Great Britain, the home of the Industrial Revolution, but there certainly was a similarity in attitude to be found in science and nascent industry. Close observation and careful generalization leading to practical utilization were characteristic of both industrialists and experimentalists alike in the 18th century. One point of direct contact is known, namely James Watt's interest in the efficiency of the Newcomen steam engine, an interest that grew from his work as a scientific-instrument maker and that led to his development of the separate condenser that made the steam engine an effective industrial power source. But in general the Industrial Revolution proceeded without much direct scientific help. Yet the potential influence of science was to prove of fundamental importance.

What science offered in the 18th century was the hope that careful observation and experimentation might improve industrial production significantly. In some areas, it did. The potter Josiah Wedgwood built his successful business on the basis of careful study of clays and glazes and by the invention of instruments such as the pyrometer with which to gauge and control the processes he employed. It was not, however, until the second half of the 19th century that science was able to provide truly significant help to industry. It was then that the science of metallurgy permitted the tailoring of alloy steels to industrial specifications, that the science of chemistry permitted the creation of new substances, such as the aniline dyes, of fundamental industrial importance, and that electricity and magnetism were harnessed in the electric dynamo and motor. Until that period science probably profited more from industry than the other way around. It was the steam engine that posed the problems that led, by way of a search for a theory of steam power, to the creation of thermodynamics. Most importantly, as industry required ever more complicated and intricate machinery, the machine tool industry developed to provide it and, in the process, made possible the construction of ever more delicate and refined instruments for science. As science turned from the everyday world to the worlds of atoms and molecules, electric currents and magnetic fields, microbes and viruses, and nebulae and galaxies, instruments increasingly provided the sole contact with phenomena. A large refracting telescope driven by intricate clockwork to observe nebulae was as much a product of 19th-century heavy industry as were the steam locomotive and the steamship.

The Industrial Revolution had one further important effect on the development of modern science. The prospect of applying science to the problems of industry served to stimulate public support for science. The first great scientific school of the modern world, the École

Polytechnique in Paris, was founded in 1794 to put the results of science in the service of France. The founding of scores more technical schools in the 19th and 20th centuries encouraged the widespread diffusion of scientific knowledge and provided further opportunity for scientific advance. Governments, in varying degrees and at different rates, began supporting science even more directly, by making financial grants to scientists, by founding research institutes, and by bestowing honours and official posts on great scientists. By the end of the 19th century the natural philosopher following his private interests had given way to the professional scientist with a public role.

# THE ROMANTIC REVOLT

Perhaps inevitably, the triumph of Newtonian mechanics elicited a reaction, one that had important implications for the further development of science. Its origins are many and complex, and notably include one associated with the German philosopher Immanuel Kant. Kant challenged the Newtonian confidence that the scientist can deal directly with subsensible entities such as atoms, the corpuscles of light, or electricity. Instead, Kant insisted, all that the human mind can know is forces. This epistemological axiom freed Kantians from having to conceive of forces as embodied in specific and immutable particles. It also placed new emphasis on the space between particles; indeed, if one eliminated the particles entirely, there remained only space containing forces. From these two considerations were to come powerful arguments, first, for the transformations and conservation of forces and, second, for field theory as a representation of reality. What makes this point of view Romantic is that the idea of a network of forces in space tied the cosmos into a

*Immanuel Kant.* DEA Picture Library/Getty Images

unity in which all forces were related to all others, so that the universe took on the aspect of a cosmic organism. The whole was greater than the sum of all its parts, and the way to truth was contemplation of the whole, not analysis.

What Romantics, or nature philosophers, as they called themselves, could see that was hidden from their Newtonian colleagues was demonstrated by Hans Christian Ørsted. He found it impossible to believe that there was no connection between the forces of nature. Chemical affinity, electricity, heat, magnetism, and light must, he argued, simply be different manifestations of the basic forces of attraction and repulsion. In 1820 he showed that electricity and magnetism were related, for the passage of an electrical current through a wire affected a nearby magnetic needle. This fundamental discovery was explored and exploited by Michael Faraday, who spent his whole scientific life converting one force into another. By concentrating on the patterns of forces produced by electric currents and magnets, Faraday laid the foundations for field theory, in which the energy of a system was held to be spread throughout the system and not localized in real or hypothetical particles.

The transformations of force necessarily raised the question of the conservation of force. Is anything lost when electrical energy is turned into magnetic energy, or into heat or light or chemical affinity or mechanical power? Faraday, again, provided one of the early answers in his two laws of electrolysis, based on experimental observations that quite specific amounts of electrical "force" decomposed quite specific amounts of chemical substances. This work was followed by that of James Prescott Joule, Robert Mayer, and Hermann von Helmholtz, each of whom arrived at a generalization of basic importance to all science, the principle of the conservation of energy.

The nature philosophers were primarily experimentalists who produced their transformations of forces by clever experimental manipulation. The exploration of the nature of elemental forces benefitted as well from the rapid development of mathematics. In the 19th century the study of heat was transformed into the science of thermodynamics, based firmly on mathematical analysis; the Newtonian corpuscular theory of light was replaced by Augustin-Jean Fresnel's mathematically sophisticated undulatory theory; and the phenomena of electricity and magnetism were distilled into succinct mathematical form by William Thomson (Lord Kelvin) and James Clerk Maxwell. By the end of the century, thanks to the principle of the conservation of energy and the second law of thermodynamics, the physical world appeared to be completely comprehensible in terms of complex but precise mathematical forms describing various mechanical transformations in some underlying ether.

The submicroscopic world of material atoms became similarly comprehensible in the 19th century. Beginning with John Dalton's fundamental assumption that atomic species differ from one another solely in their weights, chemists were able to identify an increasing number of elements and to establish the laws describing their interactions. Order was established by arranging elements according to their atomic weights and their reactions. The result was the periodic table, devised by Dmitry Mendeleyev, which implied that some kind of subatomic structure underlay elemental qualities. That structure could give rise to qualities, thus fulfilling the prophecy of the 17th-century mechanical philosophers, was shown in the 1870s by Joseph-Achille Le Bel and Jacobus van't Hoff, whose studies of organic chemicals showed the correlation between the arrangement of atoms or groups of atoms in space and specific chemical and physical properties.

# ELEMENTS

| | | W.t | | | | W.t |
|---|---|---|---|---|---|---|
| ⊙ | Hydrogen. | 1 | ⊕ | Strontian | 46 |
| ⊖ | Azote | 5 | ✳ | Barytes | 68 |
| ● | Carbon | 54 | Ⓘ | Iron | 50 |
| ○ | Oxygen | 7 | Ⓩ | Zinc | 56 |
| ☮ | Phosphorus | 9 | Ⓒ | Copper | 56 |
| ⊕ | Sulphur | 13 | Ⓛ | Lead | 90 |
| | Magnesia | 20 | Ⓢ | Silver | 190 |
| | Lime | 24 | Ⓖ | Gold | 190 |
| ⊖ | Soda | 28 | Ⓟ | Platina | 190 |
| | Potash | 42 | | Mercury | 167 |

English meteorologist and chemist John Dalton's table of elements, c. 1808. Dalton was a pioneer in the development of modern atomic theory. **Science & Society Picture Library/ Getty Images**

# PERIODIC TABLE

The periodic table is an organized array of all the chemical elements in approximately increasing order of their atomic weight. The elements show a periodic recurrence of certain properties, first discovered in 1869 by Dmitry I. Mendeleyev. Those in the same column (group) of the table as usually arranged have similar properties. In the 20th century, when the structure of atoms was understood, the table was seen to precisely reflect increasing order of atomic number. Members of the same group in the table have the same number of electrons in the outermost shells of their atoms and form bonds of the same type, usually with the same valence; the noble gases, with full outer shells, generally do not form bonds. The periodic table has thus greatly deepened understanding of bonding and chemical behaviour. It also allowed the prediction of new elements, many of which were later discovered or synthesized.

**Periodic Table of the Elements**

| Ia | | | | | | | | | | | | | | | | | zero |
|----|----|----|----|----|----|----|----|----|----|----|----|----|----|----|----|----|----|
| 1 H | IIa | | | | | | | | | | | IIIa | IVa | Va | VIa | VIIa | 2 He |
| 3 Li | 4 Be | | | | | | | | | | | 5 B | 6 C | 7 N | 8 O | 9 F | 10 Ne |
| 11 Na | 12 Mg | IIIb | IVb | Vb | VIb | VIIb | ←—VIIIb—→ | | | Ib | IIb | 13 Al | 14 Si | 15 P | 16 S | 17 Cl | 18 Ar |
| 19 K | 20 Ca | 21 Sc | 22 Ti | 23 V | 24 Cr | 25 Mn | 26 Fe | 27 Co | 28 Ni | 29 Cu | 30 Zn | 31 Ga | 32 Ge | 33 As | 34 Se | 35 Br | 36 Kr |
| 37 Rb | 38 Sr | 39 Y | 40 Zr | 41 Nb | 42 Mo | 43 Tc | 44 Ru | 45 Rh | 46 Pd | 47 Ag | 48 Cd | 49 In | 50 Sn | 51 Sb | 52 Te | 53 I | 54 Xe |
| 55 Cs | 56 Ba | 57 La | 72 Hf | 73 Ta | 74 W | 75 Re | 76 Os | 77 Ir | 78 Pt | 79 Au | 80 Hg | 81 Tl | 82 Pb | 83 Bi | 84 Po | 85 At | 86 Rn |
| 87 Fr | 88 Ra | 89 Ac | 104 Rf | 105 Db | 106 Sg | 107 Bh | 108 Hs | 109 Mt | 110 Ds | 111 Rg | 112 Cn | 113 (Uut) | 114 (Uuq) | 115 (Uup) | 116 (Uuh) | 117 (Uus) | 118 (Uuo) |

| lanthanoid series | 58 Ce | 59 Pr | 60 Nd | 61 Pm | 62 Sm | 63 Eu | 64 Gd | 65 Tb | 66 Dy | 67 Ho | 68 Er | 69 Tm | 70 Yb | 71 Lu |
|---|---|---|---|---|---|---|---|---|---|---|---|---|---|---|
| actinoid series | 90 Th | 91 Pa | 92 U | 93 Np | 94 Pu | 95 Am | 96 Cm | 97 Bk | 98 Cf | 99 Es | 100 Fm | 101 Md | 102 No | 103 Lr |

H hydrogen  Fe iron  Ag silver  Au gold  C carbon  O oxygen

Discoveries of elements 113–118 are claimed but not confirmed.

© 2011 Encyclopædia Britannica, Inc.

*The periodic table groups elements by their properties.*
**Encyclopædia Britannica, Inc.**

# THE FOUNDING OF MODERN BIOLOGY

The study of living matter lagged far behind physics and chemistry, largely because organisms are so much more complex than inanimate bodies or forces. William Harvey had shown that living matter could be studied experimentally, but his achievement stood alone for two centuries. For the time being, most students of living nature had to be content to classify living forms as best they could and to attempt to isolate and study aspects of living systems.

As has been seen, an avalanche of new specimens in both botany and zoology put severe pressure on taxonomy. A giant step forward was taken in the 18th century by the Swedish naturalist Carl von Linné—known by his Latinized name, Linnaeus—who introduced a rational, if somewhat artificial, system of binomial nomenclature. The very artificiality of Linnaeus's system, focussing as it did on only a few key structures, encouraged criticism and attempts at more natural systems. The attention thus called to the organism as a whole reinforced a growing intuition that species are linked in some kind of genetic relationship, an idea first made scientifically explicit by Jean-Baptiste, chevalier de Lamarck.

Problems encountered in cataloging the vast collection of invertebrates at the Museum of Natural History in Paris led Lamarck to suggest that species change through time. This idea was not so revolutionary as it is usually painted, for, although it did upset some Christians who read the book of Genesis literally, naturalists who noted the shading of natural forms one into another had been toying with the notion for some time. Lamarck's system failed to gain general assent largely because it relied upon an antiquated chemistry for its causal agents and appeared to imply a conscious drive to perfection on the part of organisms. It was also opposed by one of the most powerful paleontologists

*Jean-Baptiste Lamarck.* **Stock Montage/Archive Photos/ Getty Images**

and comparative anatomists of the day, Georges Cuvier, who happened to take Genesis quite literally. In spite of Cuvier's opposition, however, the idea remained alive and was finally elevated to scientific status by the labours of Charles Darwin. Darwin not only amassed a wealth of data supporting the notion of transformation of species, but he also was able to suggest a mechanism by which such evolution could occur without recourse to other than purely natural causes. The mechanism was natural selection, according to which minute variations in offspring were either favoured or eliminated in the competition for survival, and it permitted the idea of evolution to be perceived with great clarity. Nature shuffled and sorted its own productions, through processes governed purely by chance, so that those organisms that survived were better adapted to a constantly changing environment.

Darwin's *On the Origin of Species by Means of Natural Selection, or the Preservation of Favoured Races in the Struggle for Life*, published in 1859, brought order to the world of organisms. A similar unification at the microscopic level had been brought about by the cell theory announced by Theodor Schwann and Matthias Schleiden in 1838, whereby cells were held to be the basic units of all living tissues. Improvements in the microscope during the 19th century made it possible gradually to lay bare the basic structures of cells, and rapid progress in biochemistry permitted the intimate probing of cellular physiology. By the end of the century the general feeling was that physics and chemistry sufficed to describe all vital functions and that living matter, subject to the same laws as inanimate matter, would soon yield up its secrets. This reductionist view was triumphantly illustrated in the work of Jacques Loeb, who showed that so-called instincts in lower animals are nothing more than physicochemical reactions, which he labelled tropisms.

*Charles Darwin, c. 1870.* **Library of Congress Prints and Photographs Division**

The most dramatic revolution in 19th-century biology was the one created by the germ theory of disease, championed by Louis Pasteur in France and Robert Koch in Germany. Through their investigations, bacteria were shown to be the specific causes of many diseases. By means of immunological methods first devised by Pasteur, some of mankind's chief maladies were brought under control.

# TROPISM

Tropism is the response or orientation of a plant or certain lower animals to a stimulus that acts with greater intensity from one direction than another. It may be achieved by active movement or by structural alteration. Forms of tropism include phototropism (response to light), geotropism (response to gravity), chemotropism (response to particular substances), hydrotropism (response to water), thigmotropism (response to mechanical stimulation), traumatotropism (response to wound lesion), and galvanotropism, or electrotropism (response to electric current). Most tropic movements are orthotropic; i.e., they are directed toward the source of the stimulus. Plagiotropic movements are oblique to the direction of stimulus. Diatropic movements are at right angles to the direction of stimulus.

*Two plants display phototropism in action as they reach toward the sun.* **Hope Lourie Killcoyne**

# THE 20TH-CENTURY REVOLUTION AND BEYOND

**B**y the end of the 19th century, the dream of the mastery of nature for the benefit of mankind, first expressed in all its richness by Sir Francis Bacon, seemed on the verge of realization. Science was moving ahead on all fronts, reducing ignorance and producing new tools for the amelioration of the human condition. A comprehensible, rational view of the world was gradually emerging from laboratories and universities. One savant went so far as to express pity for those who would follow him and his colleagues, for they, he thought, would have nothing more to do than to measure things to the next decimal place.

But this sunny confidence did not last long. One annoying problem was that the radiation emitted by atoms proved increasingly difficult to reduce to known mechanical principles. More importantly, physics found itself relying more and more upon the hypothetical properties of a substance, the *ether*, which stubbornly eluded detection. Within a span of 10 short years, roughly 1895–1905, these and related problems came to a head and wrecked the mechanistic system the 19th century had so laboriously built. The discovery of

X rays and radioactivity revealed an unexpected new complexity in the structure of atoms. Max Planck's solution to the problem of thermal radiation introduced a discontinuity into the concept of energy that was inexplicable in terms of classical thermodynamics. Most disturbing of all, the enunciation of the special theory of relativity by Albert Einstein in 1905 not only destroyed the ether and all the physics that depended on it but also redefined physics as the study of relations between observers and events, rather than of the events themselves. What was observed, and therefore what happened, was now said to be a function of the observer's location and motion relative to other events. Absolute space was a fiction. The very foundations of physics threatened to crumble.

# ETHER

Ether (also spelled aether, also called luminiferous ether) in physics, is a theoretical, universal substance believed during the 19th century to have acted as the medium for transmission of electromagnetic waves (e.g., light and X rays) much as sound waves are transmitted by elastic media such as air. The ether was assumed to be weightless, transparent, frictionless, undetectable chemically or physically, and literally permeating all matter and space. The theory met with increasing difficulties as the nature of light and the structure of matter became better understood; it was seriously weakened (1881) by the Michelson-Morley experiment, which was designed specifically to detect the motion of the Earth through the ether and which showed that there was no such effect.

With the formulation of the special theory of relativity by Albert Einstein in 1905 and its acceptance by scientists generally, the ether hypothesis was abandoned as being unnecessary in terms of Einstein's assumption that the speed of light, or any electromagnetic wave, is a universal constant.

This modern revolution in physics has not yet been fully assimilated by historians of science. Suffice it to say that scientists managed to come to terms with all of the upsetting results of early 20th-century physics but in ways that made the new physics utterly different from the old. Mechanical models were no longer acceptable, because there were processes (such as light) for which no consistent model could be constructed. No longer could physicists speak with confidence of physical reality, but only of the probability of making certain measurements.

# Science in the 21st Century: The Search for the Higgs Boson

The Higgs boson, also called the Higgs particle, is a hypothetical particle that is postulated to be the carrier particle, or boson, of the Higgs field, a theoretical field that permeates space and endows all elementary subatomic particles with mass through its interactions with them. The field and the particle—named after Peter Higgs of the University of Edinburgh, one of the physicists who first proposed this mechanism—provide a testable hypothesis for the origin of mass in elementary particles.

On July 4, 2012, scientists at the Large Hadron Collider (LHC), a particle accelerator at the European Organization for Nuclear Research (CERN) near Geneva, announced that the decades-long search for the Higgs boson was over. Two different experiments, ATLAS (A Toroidal LHC Apparatus) and CMS (Compact Muon Solenoid), had detected a particle with a mass of 125 billion–126 billion electron volts (GeV) that was almost certainly a Higgs boson. Further data would be needed to confirm the observations, but if they were accurate, then the CERN researchers would have found the particle excitation of the Higgs field, which permeates all space and endows

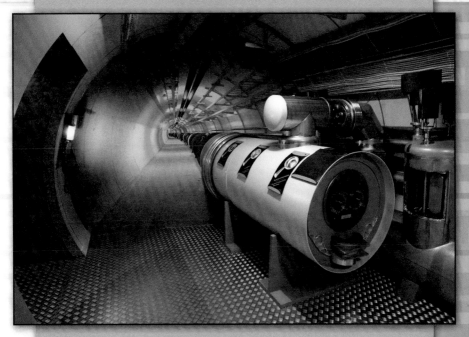

*A model of the Large Hadron Collider (LHC) tunnel on view in the CERN (European Organization for Nuclear Research) visitors' centre, in Geneva-Meyrin, Switzerland, June 2008.* **Johannes Simon/Getty Images**

subatomic particles with mass. In popular culture the Higgs boson had come to be called the "God particle," after Nobel physicist Leon Lederman's book, *The God Particle: If the Universe Is the Answer, What Is the Question?* (1993), which asserted that discovering the particle was crucial to a final understanding of the structure of matter.

There is still no doubt that science in the 20th and 21st centuries have worked wonders. The new physics—relativity, quantum mechanics, particle physics—may outrage common sense, but it enables physicists to probe to the very limits of physical reality. Their instruments and mathematics permit modern scientists to manipulate subatomic particles with relative ease, to reconstruct the first moment of creation, and to glimpse dimly the grand structure and ultimate fate of the universe.

The revolution in physics has spilled over into chemistry and biology and led to hitherto undreamed-of capabilities for the manipulation of atoms and molecules and of cells and their genetic structures. Chemists perform molecular tailoring today as a matter of course, cutting and shaping molecules at will. Genetic engineering makes possible active human intervention in the evolutionary process and holds out the possibility of tailoring living organisms, including the human organism, to specific tasks. This second scientific revolution may prove to be, for good or ill, the most important event in the history of mankind.

**alchemy** A theoretical system that involved the effort to change lead into gold.

**antipodes** The parts of Earth diametrically opposite from each other.

**apogee** The highest point of development.

**argot** An often more or less secret vocabulary and idiom peculiar to a particular group.

**Beaker folk** Late Neolithic–Early Bronze Age people living about 4,500 years ago in the temperate zones of Europe; they received their name from their distinctive bell-shaped beakers, decorated in horizontal zones by finely toothed stamps.

**Boyle's law** Statement in physics: the volume of a gas at constant temperature varies inversely with the pressure exerted on it.

**canon** Any comprehensive list of books within a field or genre.

**causation** The relation between a cause and its effect or between regularly correlated events or phenomena.

**cist** A neolithic or Bronze Age burial chamber typically lined with stone.

**construct** A theoretical entity or a product of ideology, history, or social circumstances.

**cyclopean** Of or relating to a style of stone construction marked typically by the use of large irregular blocks without mortar.

**dictum** A statement made with authority.

**epicycle** A small circle, the centre of which moves on the circumference of a larger circle at whose centre is Earth.

**epistemological** The study or a theory of the nature and grounds of knowledge especially with reference to its limits and validity.

**epochal** Uniquely or highly significant; unparalleled.

**Godhead** Divine nature or essence; divinity.

**Hellenophile** One who loves Greek culture.

**Hermetic** Of or relating to the Gnostic writings or teachings arising in the first three centuries CE and attributed to Hermes Trismegistos.

**Jehovah** Judeo-Christian name for God, derived from Yahweh.

**Marduk** In Mesopotamian religion, the chief god of the city of Babylon and the national god of Babylonia; as such, he was eventually called simply Bel, or Lord.

**megalithic** Of or relating to large, usually rough stone used in prehistoric cultures as a monument or building block.

**monochord** An instrument of ancient origin for measuring and demonstrating the mathematical relations of musical tones that consists of a single string stretched over a sound box and a movable bridge set on a graduated scale.

**novae** Stars that suddenly increase greatly in brightness and then within a few months or years grow dim again.

**presage** To warn or suggest of future events.

**protoscience** An area of inquiry that predated the modern scientific method but eventually gave way to a modern science.

**puerility** Showing a lack of maturity, seriousness, or good judgment.

**Pythagorean theorem** Rule relating the lengths of the sides of a right triangle.

**savant** A scholar.

**torsion** The twisting or wrenching of a body by the exertion of forces tending to turn one end or part about a longitudinal axis while the other is held fast or turned in the opposite direction.

**verisimilitude** The appearance of being true or real.

# BIBLIOGRAPHY

## GENERAL WORKS

George Sarton, *A History of Science*, 2 vol. (1952–59, reissued 1993), and *Introduction to the History of Science*, 3 vol. in 5 (1927–48, reprinted 1975), embody the legacy of this founder of the discipline of the history of science. Though more philosophical in tone, the immensely influential work by Thomas Kuhn, *The Structure of Scientific Revolutions*, 3rd ed. (1996), is essential reading for the student of the history of science. Of several surveys of the entire field, J.D. Bernal, *Science in History*, new ed., 4 vol. (1969, reissued 1979), although Marxist-inflected, is the most easily accessible and useful—vol. 1 and 2 are the strongest. David C. Lindberg, *The Beginnings of Western Science* (1992), is the best recent overview of Western science to 1400, with a thorough bibliography. Joseph Needham et al., *Science and Civilisation in China* (1954– ), is the indispensable history of Chinese science and technology; Colin Ronan, *The Shorter Science and Civilisation in China* (1980– ), is an abridgment.

General studies of specific fields include Dirk J. Struik, *A Concise History of Mathematics*, 4th rev. ed. (1987); Dirk J. Struik (ed.), *A Source Book in Mathematics*, 1200–1800 (1969, reprinted 1986); on astronomy, Timothy Ferris, *Coming of Age in the Milky Way* (1988); and John North, *The Fontana History of Astronomy and Cosmology* (also published as *The Norton History of Astronomy and Cosmology*, 1994); Peter J. Bowler, *The Fontana History of the Environmental Sciences* (1992; also published as *The Norton History of the Environmental Sciences*, 1993). The relationship between science and religion is surveyed in John Hedley Brooke, *Science and Religion: Some Historical Perspectives* (1991); and David C. Lindberg and Ronald L. Numbers (eds.), *God and Nature* (1986), a valuable collection of historical essays.

Charles Coulton Gillispie (ed.), *Dictionary of Scientific Biography*, 16 vol. (1970–80), is the definitive biographical reference source for the field. Roy Porter (ed.), *The Biographical Dictionary of Scientists*, 2nd ed. (1994), offers briefer biographies. A series of annotated bibliographies of literature on the history of science and technology includes, for example, Gavin Bridson, *The History of Natural History* (1994); Bernard S. Finn, *The History of Electrical Technology* (1991); and David F. Channell, *The History of Engineering Science* (1989). *Isis Current Bibliography of the History of Science and Its Cultural Influences* (annual) surveys the most recent literature.

Ongoing research is reported in a number of journals. *Isis* (quarterly) is the leading U.S. journal; and *Osiris* (annual) is also published in the United States; while *History of Science* (quarterly) and *The British Journal for the History of Science* (quarterly) are good British journals with wide coverage, bibliographies, and essay reviews. More specialized journals include *Historical Studies in the Physical and Biological Sciences* (semiannual); *Journal of the History of Biology* (3/yr.); *Journal for the History of Astronomy* (quarterly); *Ambix* (3/yr.), on the history of chemistry and alchemy; *Studies in History and Philosophy of Science* (quarterly); and *Social Studies of Science* (quarterly).

# ANCIENT AND MEDIEVAL SCIENCE

Mott T. Greene, *Natural Knowledge in Preclassical Antiquity* (1992), is a general survey of preclassical sciences; while O. Neugebauer, *The Exact Sciences in Antiquity*, 2nd ed. (1957, reissued 1993), focuses on ancient mathematics and astronomy. The best general history of Greek science is G.E.R. Lloyd, *Early Greek Science: Thales to Aristotle* (1970), and *Greek Science After Aristotle* (1973); Marshall Clagett, *Greek Science in Antiquity* (1955, reissued 1994), is also of value. G.E.R. Lloyd, *Adversaries and Authorities* (1996), is a comparative study of Greek and Chinese science. Roman science is treated in William H. Stahl, *Roman Science: Origins, Development, and Influence to the Later Middle Ages* (1962, reprinted 1978); and Roger French and Frank Greenaway (eds.), *Science in the Early Roman Empire: Pliny the Elder, His Sources and Influences* (1986).

There is no book-length survey of Islamic science, but A.I. Sabra, "Science, Islamic," in Joseph R. Strayer (ed.), *Dictionary of the Middle Ages* (1988), vol. 11, pp. 81–89, is a good short overview. Astronomy and physics are discussed in A.I. Sabra, *Optics, Astronomy, and Logic: Studies in Arabic Science and Philosophy* (1994); David A. King, *Astronomy in the Service of Islam* (1993); and Edward Grant, *Planets, Stars, and Orbs: The Medieval Cosmos*, 1200–1687 (1994). Toby E. Huff, *The Rise of Early Modern Science* (1993), compares science in the medieval Islamic world, China, and the West. A.C. Crombie, *Augustine to Galileo*, 2nd rev. ed., 2 vol. (1959, reissued as *The History of Science from Augustine to Galileo*, 2 vol. in 1, 1995), is still a useful introduction to medieval science. Edward Grant, *Physical Science in the Middle Ages* (1971); and Marshall Clagett, *The Science of Mechanics in the Middle Ages* (1959, reissued 1979), discuss medieval physics. Lynn White, "The Historical Roots of Our Ecological Crisis," *Science*, 155:1203–07 (March 10, 1967), presents an influential argument about medieval attitudes toward nature. Joyce E. Salisbury, *The Beast Within* (1994), discusses medieval attitudes toward animals.

# THE SCIENTIFIC REVOLUTION

The vast literature on the scientific revolution is surveyed in H. Floris Cohen, *The Scientific Revolution: A*

*Historiographical Inquiry* (1994). Allen G. Debus, *Man and Nature in the Renaissance* (1978); and Steven Shapin, *The Scientific Revolution* (1996), are the best short overviews. Additional surveys include Margaret C. Jacob, *The Cultural Meaning of the Scientific Revolution* (1988, reissued 1993), strong on comparative and social issues; David C. Lindberg and Robert S. Westman (eds.), *Reappraisals of the Scientific Revolution* (1990), a cross section of current scholarship; and A. Rupert Hall, *The Scientific Revolution, 1500–1800: The Formation of the Modern Scientific Attitude*, 2nd ed. (1962, reissued 1972), a classic intellectual history. The relationship between science, politics, and society in early modern England has been the subject of numerous important studies, including Robert K. Merton, *Science, Technology & Society in Seventeenth Century England* (1938, reissued 1993), which argues for a "Puritan spur to science"; while Charles Webster, *The Great Instauration: Science, Medicine, and Reform, 1626–1660* (1975), presents a case for more radical interest in science in England. Steven Shapin and Simon Schaffer, *Leviathan and the Air-Pump: Hobbes, Boyle, and the Experimental Life* (1985); and Steven Shapin, *A Social History of Truth: Civility and Science in Seventeenth-Century England* (1994), trace the development of the experimental method. Samuel Y. Edgerton, Jr., *The Heritage of Giotto's Geometry* (1991), explores the relationship between art and science in the Renaissance. Physical science and astronomy are discussed in Alexandre Koyré, *From the Closed World to the Infinite Universe* (1957, reissued 1994); Thomas S. Kuhn, *The Copernican Revolution: Planetary Astronomy in the Development of Western Thought* (1957, reissued 1985); and Richard S. Westfall, *The Construction of Modern Science: Mechanisms and Mechanics* (1971). Natural history and biology are treated in Martin J.S. Rudwick, *The Meaning of Fossils: Episodes in the History of Palaeontology*, 2nd rev. ed.

(1976, reprinted 1985). The links between Hermeticism, magic, and science are explored in Frances A. Yates, *Giordano Bruno and the Hermetic Tradition* (1964, reissued 1991); Keith Thomas, *Religion and the Decline of Magic* (1971); and Brian Vickers (ed.), *Occult and Scientific Mentalities in the Renaissance* (1984). Alchemy is examined in Betty Jo Teeter Dobbs, *The Janus Faces of Genius: The Role of Alchemy in Newton's Thought* (1991); William R. Newman, *Gehennical Fire: The Lives of George Starkey, an American Alchemist in the Scientific Revolution* (1994); and Pamela H. Smith, *The Business of Alchemy: Science and Culture in the Holy Roman Empire* (1994). Studies of gender and Renaissance science include Evelyn Fox Keller, *Reflections on Gender and Science* (1985, reissued 1995), an essential starting point; Carolyn Merchant, *The Death of Nature: Women, Ecology, and the Scientific Revolution* (1980, reissued 1990); and the controversial work by David F. Noble, *A World Without Women: The Christian Clerical Culture of Western Science* (1992).

# MODERN SCIENCE

Thomas L. Hankins, *Science and the Enlightenment* (1985), is an excellent survey of 18th-century science. Joseph Ben-David, *The Scientist's Role in Society* (1971, reprinted with a new introduction, 1984), surveys the development of scientific institutions and communities in Europe and America. Margaret C. Jacob (ed.), *The Politics of Western Science, 1640–1990* (1994); and Peter Galison and Bruce Hevly (eds.), *Big Science: The Growth of Large-Scale Research* (1992), are useful introductions to the politics of science. Works on gender and science include Margaret Alic, *Hypatia's Heritage: A History of Women in Science from Antiquity Through the Nineteenth Century* (1986), which is strongest on the modern period; Londa L. Schiebinger, *Nature's Body: Gender in the Making of Modern Science* (1993); Ludmilla Jordanova, *Sexual Visions: Images of Gender in Science and Medicine Between the Eighteenth and Twentieth Centuries* (1989, reissued 1993); and Margaret W. Rossiter, *Women Scientists in America: Struggles and Strategies to 1940* (1982), and *Women Scientists in America: Before Affirmative Action, 1940–1972* (1995). Surveys of science in the national and imperial context include Nancy Stepan, *Beginnings of Brazilian Science* (1976, reissued 1981); Lewis Pyenson, *Cultural Imperialism and the Exact Sciences: German Expansion Overseas, 1900–1930* (1985); Daniel R. Headrick, *The Tentacles of Progress: Technology Transfer in the Age of Imperialism, 1850–1940* (1988); James R. Bartholomew, *The Formation of Science in Japan* (1989); and Loren R. Graham, *Science in Russia and the Soviet Union* (1993).

The literature on specific sciences since the 18th century is voluminous. The physical sciences are discussed in J.L. Heilbron, *Electricity in the 17th and 18th Centuries* (1979); Christa Jungnickel and Russell McCormmach, *Intellectual Mastery of Nature: Theoretical Physics from Ohm to Einstein*, 2 vol. (1986), strong on the late 19th century; Daniel J. Kevles, *The Physicists* (1978, reprinted 1995), a history of American physics; P.M. Harman, *Energy, Force, and Matter* (1982), on 19th-century developments; and three important collections of essays: Peter Galison, *How Experiments End* (1987), on high-energy physics; David Gooding, Trevor Pinch, and Simon Schaffer (eds.), *The Uses of Experiment: Studies in the Natural Sciences* (1989); and Jed Z. Buchwald (ed.), *Scientific Practice: Theories and Stories of Doing Physics* (1995). Henry C. King, *The History of the Telescope* (1955, reprinted 1979), is still useful as a history of astronomy; while Owen Gingerich (ed.), *Astrophysics and Twentieth-Century Astronomy to 1950*, vol. 1 (1984), is a more recent survey.

Karl Hufbauer, *Exploring the Sun: Solar Science Since Galileo* (1991), focusses on solar physics. David H. DeVorkin, *The History of Modern Astronomy and Astrophysics* (1982), is an annotated bibliographic guide. Quantification and mathematics are discussed in Tore Frängsmyr, J.L. Heilbron, and Robin E. Rider (eds.), *The Quantifying Spirit in the 18th Century* (1990); Lorraine Daston, *Classical Probability in the Enlightenment* (1988); Theodore M. Porter, *The Rise of Statistical Thinking, 1820–1900* (1986), and *Trust in Numbers: The Pursuit of Objectivity in Science and Public Life* (1995); and Joan L. Richards, *Mathematical Visions: The Pursuit of Geometry in Victorian England* (1988). Voyages of discovery are studied in Harry Woolf, *The Transits of Venus: A Study of Eighteenth-Century Science* (1959); Bernard Smith, *European Vision and the South Pacific*, 2nd ed. (1985), and *Imagining the Pacific* (1992); and William H. Goetzmann, *New Lands, New Men: America and the Second Great Age of Discovery* (1986, reissued 1995). Life sciences are discussed in David Elliston Allen, *The Naturalist in Britain* (1976, reissued 1994), a social history of natural history and collecting; W.F. Bynum, *Science and the Practice of Medicine in the Nineteenth Century* (1994); Garland E. Allen, *Life Science in the Twentieth Century* (1975), a general survey; and Ronald Rainger, Keith R. Benson, and Jane Maienschein (eds.), *The American Development of Biology* (1988, reissued 1991). Evolution is the subject of Peter J. Bowler, *Evolution: The History of an Idea*, rev. ed. (1989); and Adrian Desmond, *The Politics of Evolution: Morphology, Medicine, and Reform in Radical London* (1989, reissued 1992). Genetics and molecular biology are discussed in Horace Freeland Judson, *The Eighth Day of Creation: Makers of the Revolution in Biology* (1979); James D. Watson, *The Double Helix* (1968), available also in a critical edition ed. by Gunther S. Stent (1980), an interesting and controversial autobiographical account of the discovery of DNA structure; Adele E. Clarke and Joan H. Fujimura (eds.), *The Right Tools for the Job* (1992), on instruments and animals in 20th-century biology; and Robert E. Kohler, *From Medical Chemistry to Biochemistry* (1982), and *Lords of the Fly* (1994), on *Drosophila melanogaster* and genetics research. The social sciences are discussed in Christopher Fox, Roy Porter, and Robert Wokler (eds.), *Inventing Human Science: Eighteenth-Century Domains* (1995); Dorothy Ross, *The Origins of American Social Science* (1991); Daniel J. Kevles, *In the Name of Eugenics: Genetics and the Uses of Human Heredity* (1985, reissued 1995); George W. Stocking, Jr., *Victorian Anthropology* (1987); and Donna Haraway, *Primate Visions: Gender, Race, and Nature in the World of Modern Science* (1989), a history of primatology.

# INDEX

## A

Académie des Sciences, 51, 52–53
algebra, creation of, 25
*Almagest*, 19
Americas, early science in the, 9–10
Anaximander, 16
Archimedes, 17, 18–19, 21, 34
Aristotle, 17–18, 19, 22, 25, 31, 33, 34, 40, 42, 45, 46
astronomy
   in the classic age of science, 56
   early, 6, 7–8, 9, 11, 12, 13, 17–18, 19
   and Islam, 24, 25
   and the scientific revolution, 36–48

## B

Bacon, Sir Francis, 72
biology, founding of modern, 67–70
Black, Joseph, 56
Boyle, Robert, 50, 54
Brahe, Tycho, 40–42

## C

causation, 2
cell theory, 69
chemistry, in the classic age of science, 56–58
China, early science in, 7–8, 11, 13–14
Christianity
   and medieval Europe, 25, 27, 31–32
   and Rome, 22–23
Colbert, Jean-Baptiste, 52
Copernicus, Nicolaus, and Copernican system, 36–40, 42, 45, 46, 48

Coulomb, Charles-Augustin de, 59
Curie, Marie, 53
Cuvier, Georges, 69

## D

Dalton, John, 64
Dante Alighieri, 31–32, 33, 40
Darwin, Charles, 17, 53, 69
*De humani corporis fabrica*, 48
*De revolutionibus orbium coelestium libri VI*, 37, 39
Descartes, René, 45–46, 48
dolmen, 5

## E

Einstein, Albert, 3, 73
ether, 72, 73
Euclid, 18, 21, 40
Euclidean proof, 18
Euler, Leonhard, 55
European medieval science, 25–32
*Exercitatio Anatomica De Motu Cordis et Sanguinis in Animalibus*, 50

## F

Faraday, Michael, 63
Ficino, Marsilio, 36
field theory, 63
Fresnel, Augustin-Jean, 64

## G

Galen of Pergamum, 21, 34, 48
Galileo, 42, 44–45, 48
germ theory of disease, 70
Gilbert, William, 45
Greek science, 14–32
   Aristotle and Archimedes, 17–19